When Thunder Rolls

When Thunder Rolls

DAWN COLE

CROSSBOOKS
PUBLISHING

CrossBooks™
A Division of LifeWay
1663 Liberty Drive
Bloomington, IN 47403
www.crossbooks.com
Phone: 1-866-879-0502

First published by CrossBooks 2/22/2013

ISBN: 978-1-4627-2511-3 (sc)
ISBN: 978-1-4627-2509-0 (hc)
ISBN: 978-1-4627-2510-6 (e)

Library of Congress Control Number: 2013902068

Printed in the United States of America

This book is printed on acid-free paper.

To my Prince Charming, Jacob

Contents

Acknowledgments

To Jesus—I owe my very life to You. Thank You for holding and sustaining me through the most difficult moments I've ever known. Thank You for filling me with Your strength and enabling me to take one more step and then another and another. You are my lifeline. You've never left my side but are with me constantly. Thank You for giving Jacob to me for eight years. I loved our time together and look forward to more in heaven someday. Thank You for helping me write this book and giving me grace for the long hours and late nights. One day I will see You and speak with You face-to-face. I greatly anticipate that day. I love You.

To my Prince Charming, Jacob—you are the greatest earthly love I've ever known. What an honor to walk by your side for eight years as your wife and best friend. I miss your smile, your jokes, your hugs—all of you. I promise to keep walking through this life for the glory of Jesus. Wish you could see our children. They're doing great. You'd be proud. Your legacy will live on in them, and you'll never be forgotten. We miss you and can't wait to see you again and wrap our arms around you. We love you forever and ever.

Special Thanks

(During My Book Project)

Jan and Connie Kohl, Cindy Wolfinger, Angela Davis, Mark and Cathy Dymkoski, and all the others who helped inspire me to write this book in the first place.

My loving parents, Beth and Leo Hasse, for their encouragement to finish this momentous task.

Sarah Ratkowski and Angela Davis for helping edit my work and for all your comments and advice. Mom, thank you for the countless hours you poured over my manuscript. I couldn't have done it without you. Dad, you too.

My children who gave me advice on the title and who were patient with me as I spent a great deal of time on this project. Especially my little Lydia, who watched *Mary Poppins* over and over so Mommy could work.

Friends and family who prayed for me.

(During Jacob's illness)

Fred and Leslie Cole—Thank you for raising such a fine son to be my husband. Thank you for all your help and support during his illness, for washing fruits and veggies, moving just down the street in order to help, taking care of the children ... the list could go on and on. Your love has only continued for the children and me. Thank you for praying, loving, and caring then and now.

Beth and Leo Hasse—Mom, thank you for all the times you came from Montana to help. Your support was a blessing. Dad, thank you for all the fervent prayers you lifted up on our behalf and still do. You both have been and continue to be a constant support for us. Thank you for being such good neighbors.

Josiah and Valoree Hasse—Brother and sister, thank you for being there for us: driving our kids up from San Diego, helping in the fence project and house cleaning and cleaning my pizza-stained oven. Josiah, thank you for holding me the night Jacob died. Valoree, thank you for being with me the night Lydia was born. You guys are the best.

Eva Reeck—Thank you for being an encouragement to me, Grandma. You are very special. I'm sure Bopa and Jacob are having lot's of great conversations as they explore heaven together.

Stan and Kathie Moe—Thank you for taking our children out in your boat and giving them a good time since we couldn't. Kathie, you took such good care of Jacob. I felt the love and peace of Jesus as we sat in your office. Thank you for loving us so much.

Bill and Sherron Ramich—Thank you for the countless hours you spent washing all those fresh fruits and veggies. Your labor of love will never be forgotten. Thank you for all the taco dinners too. Best tacos ever!

Pastor Dan and Nicole Christ—Dan, thank you for sitting with me that day in the waiting room and for coming to Mexico to visit us. Nicole, thank you for making sure we had food in the refrigerator when we returned and for the countless meals you organized during the duration of Jacob's illness. Thank you for praying and loving us through it all. You guys are very special. True friends.

Shane and Hannah Roberts—Thank you for taking care of the kids on many occasions, especially when Lydia was born. Thank you for your love and support and for coming to visit us here in Montana. Great times!

Aaron and Stacey Weimorts—Aaron, thank you for the times you stopped by to talk with Jacob when he was so sick. You didn't call first because you knew Jacob would say no. Instead you came anyway and sat with him. Thank you both for keeping the camping tradition alive with my boys. It means so much. Your love and friendship is such a blessing.

Kelly Palm and Amanda Nicholson—Thank you beyond words for the amazing makeover you performed on our home. Also, special thanks to all who donated to the cause (Women's Republican Group, etc.). It brought joy in the middle of our sorrow. Amanda, thank you for the red sign you made. What a treasure.

Rick Reiben and the youth at North Country Chapel—Thank you all for finishing our fence at our old home and then painting the inside of our new home and to all the girls who helped Valoree clean our old house. You have no idea how much you blessed us.

SRM Development at Riverstone—Thanks to all of you for the tickets to Sea World and the San Diego Zoo, for the first-class tickets back from San Diego, for the fundraiser, and all the other ways you supported us. It meant a lot.

Terri Reynolds and all the other wonderful ladies who cleaned our home.

Nicole Christ for heading up the Cole meal schedule, and thanks to all those who supplied us with delicious food.

Amanda Nicholson, Jen Sabatke, Mary Horton, Bill Langenderfer, Krista Tenney, and all the others who lovingly cared for our children.

Those who mowed our grass and took over our car upkeep. Pete, thank you.

The countless people near and far who prayed for us and sent us notes, flowers, and money during and after Jacob's illness. Thank you beyond words. Each card meant so much.

Tom and Sarah Mueller for making several trips to help me with the kids. Thank you, Sarah, for staying with us in San Diego.

Jim and Audrey Castile for opening your gorgeous home to us while we were in San Diego. It was like staying at a resort. Thank you for loving us.

If I have failed to mention anyone's name in specific, please know you are just as greatly appreciated. So many lives touched ours in a tremendous way. Your impact will never be forgotten.

(Since Jacob's Death)

The kind gentleman in the post office who reached out to us even though he didn't know us. You blessed me beyond words that day. I will treasure this memory for the rest of my life. Thank you as well to your sweet wife for writing me.

Kelly Price for coffee, prayers, and doctoring my kids. Thank you for caring. I know you understand. Thank you.

Jen Sabatke for taking Jacob's shirts and turning them into beautiful quilts for the children. Each one is a treasure.

Sarah Auten and Michael Leinen for walking through it all with me. It meant so much to have you there during those early days when the pain was so intense. Sarah, you're my girl. Jesus knew we needed each other and still do. "SOON."

My brother Ben Hasse for being such a fun uncle and sharing your space, movies, and gum with my children.

Joshua Cole for helping build our fabulous home. The campfire and hot dog roast night will always be my favorite memory.

Jonathan Cole for your help with the kids. Thank you for the retaining wall, hours spent painting trim, planting, mowing grass, and countless other projects around our new home.

All my lovely girls: Tiffany Rietema and Sarah Ratkowski, thank you for finding me. I didn't know I needed you, but Jesus did. Sandy Lorenc, Stephanie Hall, and Bonai Brizendine, thank you for loving me. Cara Dyson, your Facebook notes have come at the moments when I needed them so much. Thank you. Andrea Collins and Traci Scherer, thank you for reaching out to me. Rhonda, thank you for praying for me the first Sunday we met. Jesus sent you to me. Laura Price, thank you for being my friend. You are always willing to help with my kids.

Keith Collins, thank you for reaching into my boys' lives. It meant a lot.

Randy and Mary Campbell for all the time spent with Jacob and for offering your place in Hawaii to celebrate his recovery. Can we do a rain check on that and move the location to the ultimate Paradise where we will all celebrate together one day?

Carolyn Joslin for being the best realtor ever. I needed you!

All my Summit (Mount Zion) family for the prayers, packages, and support. You're so great.

Richard and Ella LaMarre for the continual cards, money, and fabulous surprises for the kids each Christmas. Thank you beyond words.

Steve and Jo Rietema for plowing, raking, and digging in my yard, and for bringing in extra dirt and finally planting grass seed in my front yard. A true labor of love.

Brian Tenney for excellent accountant work. Thank you.

Pat and Roni Mahar for having my kids to your house for pizza and movie night, for all the times you let them play with your kids, and for the fabulous haircuts.

Rem and Sara Kohrt for being such fabulous neighbors, for homemade bread and jam, and the Mother's Day gifts you helped the children make for me. Rem, thanks for fixing stuff at the rental.

Matt and Jenny Rohr for their amazing love and financial support. You guys are amazing. Jenny, thank you for coming to see me after Jacob died. What a delight.

Jake Suitter for doing an excellent job on the trim work. Thank you.

Dr. Dilan of Dilan Dental for coming in on your day off to look at Clayton's mouth and referring us to a trusted oral surgeon. You helped save the day.

Dr. Weber of Kalispell Oral Surgery for the "gift" of stitching you did in Clayton's mouth. Your kindness will never be forgotten.

Once again, if I've failed to mention anyone's name in specific, please know you are just as greatly appreciated. So many lives touched ours in a tremendous way. Your impact will last for a lifetime.

If You Want Me To

It may not be the way I would have chosen
When You lead me through a world that's not my home
But You never said it would be easy
You only said I'll never go alone ...
—Ginny Owens

Prologue:
The Last Smile (2009)

The room was dim, the only light being natural lighting from the windows. Although the shades were drawn, slices of sunlight still managed to find their way through. It looked like a hospital room, although it wasn't. It was our bedroom. Our bed stood in the middle of the room and directly to the left was a tall dresser with a table sitting next to it. The tops of both were loaded with various health care items—weapons of warfare to battle this horrifying cancer. Across the room stood another dresser on which sat get well cards from various people all hoping and praying for Jacob's complete recovery. The battle had been long and intense as it raged it's fury throughout my husband's body. It had almost been a year now since our world came crashing down around us with the news of malignant melanoma. We fought with the intensity of a heated battle zone. Artillery fire whizzed and whistled above us ... all around us ... everywhere as we gallantly fought on. But no matter how hard we tried to gain ground, we were pushed further and further back. We were losing ground, and there was nothing we could do about it.

Jacob sat in an overstuffed chair to the side of the room. There wasn't much left of him by this point. What once was a strong muscular man had wasted away to a mere skeleton. The day was Saturday, October 10, 2009. A hushed silence filled the room as my husband rested. A deep gripping fear latched onto me as I entered the room and saw his still form. He had been acting strangely, and I knew something was terribly wrong.

I quietly shut the door and walked to his side. He'd slipped into his own world for most the day, and I couldn't shake him from it. But now he was awake! I knelt down and rested my arms on the side of his chair. My man was the bravest I'd ever known. The pain he endured that year was more than I could describe. It ripped my heart out to see him this way; if only I could take some of his agony and bear it for him. Concerned, my eyes searched his. I didn't understand what was happening and felt so helpless. My whole world was wrapped up in this man who I loved more than life itself, and there was nothing I could do to free him from this nightmare. It just kept going on and on.

Jacob took a deep breath, slowly let out a long sigh, and placed his hand over his chest.

My heart melted. I was so afraid. "Is anything wrong?" I asked.

Not wanting me to worry, he sweetly answered, "No." He then turned his head and looked deeply into my eyes. Slowly, a beautiful smile spread across his face as if all the cherished memories of our past melted into one. All the joy, laughter, and love of a lifetime were wrapped up in his smile, the most beautiful one I had seen during his entire sickness. It was his last gift to me. Almost like he was trying to say good-bye but couldn't bring himself to actually speak the words because he knew it would pierce my heart.

Jacob's weary face was so precious and his smile full of pure devotion. I was the only woman he had ever loved, and now it was time to say good-bye. That smile was my last personal moment with him before the mist came back, clouding his mind and ability to function. In a matter of hours, he'd slip from this life and into the next.

Soon he'd be gone.

1

Prince Charming (1997)

The autumn air was uncomfortably hot as I made my way down the sidewalk leading to the dining hall. I noted the thickness in the air. Back home in Oregon, the air was lighter. This Pennsylvanian humidity was a whole new thing for me. It felt more like summer than it did fall. Obviously, it hadn't transitioned yet from one season to the next but was stuck somewhere in between. Needless to say, it was a relief to reach the air-conditioned cafeteria of the college campus where I had recently begun my freshman year.

Sooner or later, all of us experience moments that change us forever. Sometimes they are obviously recognizable, but sometimes they quietly come and go without much detection at all. Yet deep inside we feel something and slowly realize we will never be the same again.

I reached for the door handle that lunch hour and had little idea that one of those "moments" was about to occur. As far as I was concerned, it was simply a normal day with the normal routine I'd been following since I had arrived. But today would be different. I pulled the door open and walked inside.

I chose a seat at a table with several newfound friends. This was a new adventure for me; I was far from home and everything familiar. It had taken me some time to finally relax and feel comfortable.

I greeted my classmates and sat down. The cafeteria was humming with the cheerful chatter of excited students. There was a whole summer's worth of stories and adventures to be discussed between the returning students. They talked with excitement, happy to see one another again. The new students were just as eager to connect and begin new friendships.

Everyone at our table stood, and together we walked to the line forming at the entrance to the kitchen. As we waited our turn to pick up our food, we discussed the morning's events and reviewed how many more classes we had yet that afternoon.

The smell of food played with our noses and made our stomachs growl. Breakfast had been early that morning and with all the brain power we were now exerting everyone was very hungry. The line inched along.

Finally, with trays in hand, we returned to our table. As I ate, I quietly observed the room in which I sat. A large dining hall with high ceilings, it was filled with tables and chairs and, of course, students. One wall was all windows, and the view outside was lovely. Our Bible college campus was located in the countryside in Grantville, Pennsylvania, surrounded by flowing green fields, lush trees, and beautiful rolling hills. I had heard that the colors that time of year were breathtaking and was looking forward to autumn.

Before long, lunch was over. Students began clearing their dishes, gathering their things, and preparing for the next class. As I finished my last few bites, I again glanced around the room. Deep in the heart of every college girl is the hope that maybe, just maybe, she will meet Mr. Right while away at school, and I was not exempt from this notion. However, it was not top priority on my list. In fact, dating was against school policy. The faculty wasn't against relationships altogether; they just needed to be made and developed in the appropriate manner. Our main focus was supposed to be on our studies and all that God wanted to teach us while at school. However, I still kept my secret dream safely tucked away, hoping that one day I would find my soul mate. And what better place to find him?

Suddenly, something across the room caught my attention. A tall, handsome man rose from his chair, picked up his empty tray, and walked across the room, obviously finished with lunch and returning his dishes to the kitchen. I couldn't help but stare. I had never seen anyone so adorable in my entire life. If this wasn't Prince Charming himself then I didn't know who could be. I continued gawking at him, following his every move. Who *was* this guy? Where was he from? What was his name? Something about him instantly captured my heart. He soon finished what he was doing, turned, walked out the door, and was gone.

As I gathered my dishes and carried them to the kitchen, I was unaware of the significance of what had happened. I had no idea what a great impact this man would soon have on my life. I was oblivious that I had just seen the man I would one day marry. If I had been able to peer into my destiny, I would have jumped for joy and cowered in dread at the same time.

I would have seen a beautiful summer day with a bride and groom kissing at sunset. I would have seen many happy times and the birth of four precious babies. I would have heard laughter and the cheerful chatter of a beautiful, happy family ... but I would also have observed the inside of an operating room with a surgeon bending over my husband. I would have seen many terrible moments and heard the cries of a woman in great distress. I would have seen a cold, granite headstone with my husband's name on it.

Together we would one day experience the heights of happiness but also the depths of sorrow. We would experience all the best in life as two people in love and yet also discover the searing pain that often accompanies that love. Both mountaintops and valley gorges were to be a part of God's design for us.

God was going to provide many opportunities along the way to build and strengthen our faith in Him. And in the end, we'd be put to the ultimate test and asked, "Will you trust Me even though you don't understand what I am doing? Will you keep holding My hand

and not let go even though you don't understand the 'why' of what I allow into your life?"

Yes, God had a special plan in mind for the two of us, and this was just the beginning. Everything would unfold in due time. But for now, it was all still a mystery to me as I headed out the cafeteria door and back into the heat.

2

Jacob Cole

It wasn't difficult to discover more about Prince Charming, as he'd become a person of interest in the female world on campus. His name was Jacob Cole. Surprisingly, he was only seventeen. He seemed older than that with the maturity he possessed. Jacob was from a small town in Idaho and had come to school with his older brother, Jonathan.

I was breaking one of my own subconscious rules by thinking twice about someone younger than me. (I was nineteen.) However, this guy broadened my narrow mind-set considerably. It didn't take me long to decide he was worth the exception. It was pretty much love at first sight. Without even knowing or trying, he had captured my heart.

Days passed. I continued observing this Jacob Cole, too shy to talk much to him. So for now, I was content to simply examine him. He had a fun sense of humor and enjoyed cracking corny jokes. His face lit up in such a way that you could tell he was getting more delight out of his joke than the person to whom he was talking. And when he laughed ... I just melted.

I admired his moral character. His standards were not his own but were the result of having a personal relationship with Jesus. Jacob knew that in order to have a truly abundant life, one had to release ownership of his own person and hand it over to Jesus Christ. Jacob was truly free. He was confident in the man the Lord had made him to be and knew his life was in good hands. This perspective radiated from him.

In all the manual projects assigned to Jacob, none were too small or too great to be completed with care and diligence. He enjoyed making others happy and serving them the best he could. There wasn't a person on campus who didn't like Jacob Cole. Staff and students alike admired him.

Jacob was athletic. He and the guys hit the gym on a regular basis, and I frequently saw him outside jogging. While the weather was still nice, exercising outside was a common pastime for students. The air was cooler at dusk, making it quite pleasant after a long day.

I took advantage of evenings like this and often went out. As the sun slipped behind the hills, the street lamps flickered on. The crickets began their evening chorus as the sky filled with stars. As I enjoyed a quiet saunter with a friend and we quietly chatted, I kept a close eye out for a tall, handsome figure. Even at a distance, Jacob's muscular frame was not hard to spot.

As autumn progressed, a chill entered the air and frost formed on every blade of grass and each golden leaf. The blazing colors of autumn soon faded to dull brown, and the leaves began to fall. With the first snow, our campus turned into a white wonderland, and it was time to bring out the winter gear. The temperatures dropped to a chilling level, but that didn't stop Jacob from spending time outdoors.

He'd pull on his boots and jacket and head out into the acres of rolling fields. He loved being alone way out there spending time with Jesus, who was not only Jacob's Savior but his best friend as well. As any earthly friendship grows the more time is invested into it, so it is with God. Jacob knew that in order to remain strong in his faith, he needed to spend quality time with the Source from which it came.

Jacob wore a bright yellow and black coat on these outings, which made him easy to spot at a distance. Sometimes, I'd look out my dorm window and see a faint spot of yellow and black, and instantly I knew it was him. A smile would cross my face and a warm glow would burn in my heart. I admired him in so many ways, but this topped them all. Did he have anything about him that *wasn't* amazing? He probably did since no one is perfect, but he came pretty close.

Jacob and I were simply classmates and friends the entire rest of the year. I carried my love for him in my heart and hoped and prayed that one day Jesus would give me this amazing guy. It was like asking for the moon, but I knew if it was part of God's plan, it would happen.

Being patient wasn't always easy. I had no guarantee that my prayer would be answered to make my dream come true. I was trying very hard to stay focused on my studies. I didn't want my time at school to be wasted mooning over a guy ... I knew that by laying down my desire, I was learning to surrender my will to God. Often the greatest lessons we learn in life are not learned from words on a page but through experience. I thought I knew what was best for Jacob and me, but I recognized that God was the only one who really knew and would settle for nothing less.

3

Soul Mates in the Making (1998)

The school year was soon over, and it was time to return home. Excitement hung in the air as students prepared for summer vacation. After exchanging good-byes and hugs, we all parted ways.

I boarded the plane with mixed emotions and found my seat. I was thrilled to be going home to friends and family. The school year had been fulfilling, and I'd matured in many ways. But I felt an ache in my heart, and I knew what it was. Five simple letters, J-A-C-O-B, said it all.

Summer has a way of quickly slipping by, and before you know it, it's gone. But for me, summer couldn't go fast enough. There hadn't been a day when I didn't think of Jacob and wonder how he was and what he was doing. We had not communicated with each other over our break. We were simply friends, and as far as I knew, he had no further interest in me. However, there was always hope. And so with eager anticipation of what the future might hold, I finally found myself on the plane, heading back to school.

A classmate picked me up at the airport, and together we made the drive to campus. As we neared the campus, I couldn't stop the fluttering in my heart or calm the butterflies in my stomach. *Will Jacob already be there?* I thought to myself. It was a beautiful late-summer day, and the sky was perfectly blue. As Nate's car pulled onto the school grounds, a surge of excitement rushed through me. It was so good to be back!

The campus was crawling with activity. Students were everywhere. Some had specific agendas, but mostly they were milling about, waiting for friends to arrive.

The car stopped in front of the office, and instantly we were swarmed with hugs and hellos. It was wonderful seeing everyone again. And then, in the middle of everyone, I saw him. Jacob! He was making his way to the back of Nate's car to help unload our luggage.

My heart skipped a beat. He greeted me with a huge smile and a warm hello. As he handed me my bag, our eyes met, and I got lost in the deep blueness of his. I gathered my composure and smiled. "Hello, Jacob," I said, returning his friendly greeting.

Jacob later told me that at that instant, something within him began to stir, grabbing his attention in a new way. I had no idea, for it was only a simple greeting, but yet, right then and there, my dream was in the making. Jacob Cole was the soul mate God had chosen for me. He didn't reveal it all to him right there on the spot but rather bit by bit as Jacob was ready.

Within a few days, everyone's things were unpacked, and the school year was in full swing. My studies were going well. The love I held for Jacob only continued to increase. God used Jacob to allow me to see the reflection of my own heart. Often when we have a strong desire for something, God asks us to give it up. In this, He teaches us that nothing in our hearts should ever be more important than Him. As true followers of Christ, we need to be willing to lay anything down at anytime.

God doesn't do this to make us miserable. His love for us far surpasses our understanding, and like a father would his children, God only gives us the best. At times we may not see it for what it truly is because we can't see as God sees. However, as we choose to trust Him, we find peace in knowing He is in control, and that there is nothing to worry about. In time, He may choose to give our desires back to us, and through the process, our hearts have become stronger and more yielded to Him. But if He doesn't give them back, it means He has something far better for us and in time will help us see the wisdom of His choice. It's really a win-win situation.

As the school year progressed, I noticed that Jacob acted somewhat different toward me. He continued treating me with respect and kindness as he did every other female friend on campus. However, I began suspecting his attraction to me—something more than simply friendship. Of course, I was thrilled, and yet I was careful not to get my hopes up too high in case it didn't pan out.

One evening, as some friends and I were walking up the stairs that led from the cafeteria to the gym, Becky said, "Jacob likes you. I can tell by the way he looks at you."

"You think so?" I squealed. But I knew it was true, for my heart told me so. I walked back to the dorm that night one happy young lady. I felt as if I were walking on air. The most desirable guy on campus was interested in me! I could hardly believe it. Was my dream coming true? Could this be the one God had on "layaway" just for me?

The year pushed on from autumn to winter, and winter gave way to spring. The snow melted, and soon new life was in bloom. Tiny green shoots began forming on each tree branch. Flowers poked their way through the soil, and the grass took on a vibrant green once again. The birds sang as they warmed themselves in the sun.

By now, Jacob and I had a strong bond forming between us. During the winter months, we grew from being good friends into something far deeper. The seedling of true love was growing in our hearts, its roots digging deep into the soil of our souls. We were quickly becoming the soul mates God had been planning all along.

4

Engaged (2000–2001)

One year turned into the next, and the next turned into another. By this time, Jacob and I were completely in love. As mentioned earlier, the school did have guidelines for students in a relationship like ours. It was easy to become impatient with these strict regulations, but we realized the staff had good intentions. Besides, it was only for a season, so we made the most of it.

The two of us fit like a hand in a glove—a perfect match. We spent every spare moment together. Often in the evenings before curfew, we played a board game, cards, or simply talked. Spending downtime with Jacob was always a pleasure. He helped me relax and laugh like no one else could. Jacob won pretty consistently, game after game. But he didn't enjoy winning as much as watching my reaction to it. I was a competitive player. The more irritated I became, the more he delighted in it.

I loved Jacob's unique personality. He didn't do things the same as everyone else. He thought outside the box and blessed me in countless ways. When he first spoke of his love for me, we were sitting on a bench in the Harrisburg airport, on our way home for Christmas vacation. There was extra time to kill so, of course, we spent it together. Holding my hand, he sweetly said, "Dawn, I hold the words *I love you* with high regard. I never wanted to say them unless I really meant them, and today I do."

He reached into his bag and pulled out two wooden bears connected in the middle by a wooden heart. He told me he had carved them when he was thirteen years old. As he was working on them, he was suddenly inspired to save them and give them to the girl he wanted to spend the rest of his life with. And then he handed them to me. There wasn't a happier girl in the whole world than the one sitting there that day!

On Valentine's Day, Jacob painted a huge heart across the front of one of his T-shirts. In the middle, he wrote in capital letters, "I LOVE DAWN." He showed up at my door that morning wearing it to wish me a happy Valentine's Day and kept it on the rest of the day.

The coming of spring that year meant we were in our final days of college life. Four years had come and were nearly gone. We felt the stirring inside and grew excited with eager anticipation of the upcoming future. Without a doubt, Jacob and I knew we wanted to spend the rest of our lives together. It was time to become engaged!

Jacob had already put much thought into this special event, wanting it to be as unique as possible. We had shopped for rings together, hoping and dreaming. I knew he didn't have much money, and that the ring might have to wait. As every girl does, I dreamed of the glorious day when the man of my dreams would ask me to be his forever. It was now so close … and yet so far away.

But God has a talent for working things out in ways we can't imagine. Unbeknownst to me, Jacob had been blessed with the right amount of money he needed to buy my ring. And so with great delight, Jacob went off one Saturday morning to pick up my engagement ring from the jewelers. He carefully placed it into the beautifully handcrafted box he'd made and planned the perfect way to ask me to be his wife.

One spring day in April, the weather was overcast without a spot of blue in the gray sky, yet the temperature was pleasant. Jacob suggested a bike ride. To keep me from becoming suspicious, he asked some friends to help him stage a group event. Everyone loaded their bikes in the school van and headed to the park.

We arrived, unloaded, and set off. Before long, I noticed everyone else had vanished, leaving Jacob and me to meander down the path alone. The trail wandered beside a small stream, a truly lovely spot. Jacob and I continued riding, enjoying the day.

We came to a wooden bridge and decided to stop for a break. I sat down on the bench along the edge. Before I knew what was happening, Jacob was down on one knee, and from his pocket came the loveliest wooden heart-shaped box I'd ever seen. (He had spent hours making it.) He looked into my eyes and said the words I had been waiting so long to hear, "Dawn, will you marry me?"

He opened the box, and there on a red velvet cushion lay the beautiful engagement ring I had had my eye on. My heart skipped with joy, and I immediately said, "Yes!"

Jacob placed the ring on my finger. It fit perfectly and sparkled every time I moved my hand. I couldn't take my eyes from it and was thrilled beyond words.

That night I went to bed with a happy song in my heart. In only a matter of months, I would be Mrs. Jacob Cole. God was so good to me. I was the happiest girl in the whole world.

5

Mr. and Mrs. Jacob Cole

The months leading up to our big day were a whirl of excitement and activity. Jacob returned to Idaho to work and prepare a place for us to live while I went back to Oregon to plan our wedding. I missed him tremendously over the course of that summer, but the anticipation of becoming his wife was a reminder to my aching heart. Every couple of weeks, Jacob was able to get away for a short time and come to see me. We relished each moment together.

The wedding plans were coming along splendidly. Our venue was an English garden in Oregon. Topiaries of all sizes and shapes lined the pathways, and roses, azaleas, and all sorts of posies filled the flowerbeds. Our ceremony would take place in a glass solarium at sunset. It was truly going to be the wedding of my dreams.

At long last, our wedding day arrived. August 31, 2001. I could barely believe it was finally here! Jacob and I couldn't have been more excited. With great anticipation, we scurried around with last-minute preparations. Countless friends and family gathered to help in any way they could.

The whole day I felt like a princess preparing for the grand ball. My bridesmaids were there, busy with preparations. We fluttered about like a bunch of butterflies. The day flew by, and soon it was time for everyone to get dressed. Jacob and his groomsmen went ahead to our wedding location while the girls and I did our makeup and hair at my grandparent's house.

Little by little, the busy house quieted down as people began to leave and make their way to Talina's Garden. I was the last one in the house finishing up when I began to feel a little uneasy. The house was extremely still. Too still. Could it be possible that I was the only one left? I rushed outside just in time to see the last car pulling away. I ran over to it and shouted, "Wait!"

Shocked, my parents stopped and said, "We didn't know you were still here. We thought you were already gone!"

Well, wouldn't you know? The bride was almost left behind for her own wedding. I was thankful I ran out when I did. We certainly didn't need any delays by having to search for the bride!

The ceremony and reception were like a dream. The service opened with a time of worship, as we wanted to give honor where honor was due. Jesus was the one receiving the credit for this match. He had led us to the same school and had penned every minute of our love story with His own hand. Jacob and I couldn't have been more grateful.

Our vows were next. With great emotion, we pledged our love to one another and promised to remain faithful as long as we both lived. We assumed this would mean a full lifetime. There was no reason to believe otherwise.

The moment came to light the unity candle. We each held our small lit candle and slowly brought them together over the wick of the larger one. Instantly, it caught fire and began to glow. However, no sooner had we withdrawn our separate candles, the flame vanished. A ripple of giggles emerged from the audience as we tried to relight our candle, but to no avail. Our unity candle would not stay lit. Finally, we gave up and moved along with the service.

I'm not one to quickly label something as symbolic; however, in this instance, I wonder. Little did we both know that in eight short years our unity candle was going to flicker, flutter, and finally go out. No matter how hard we would try, it would not stay lit. However, our love would continue, for it can never die but lives on beyond the grave. Since Jacob and I had no idea what the future held, we were not affected by the candle incident on our wedding day. We only felt the happiness that continued through the rest of the ceremony and into the reception.

The time for our departure finally came. Friends and family gathered on each side of the walkway leading to our car. Instead of having our guests throw rice as we passed by, we chose for them to blow bubbles, which they did for all they were worth. Jacob and I laughed as we made our way through the cloud of popping soap.

Our car sat ready for us at the end of the line in all its grand glory of shaving cream and streamers. We hopped inside, rolled down the windows, waved, and were off to start our new life together!

6

The Golden Years (2001–2008)

The initial seven years of our marriage were an exciting journey. Jacob and I didn't stay in Idaho for long. We returned to Pennsylvania to serve as faculty members for the college where we met. It was such fun being back again, this time as husband and wife. We loved our students and fellow staff associates and were given a variety of responsibilities ranging from housekeeping to teaching. During our time off, we often hopped in the car and drove, as there was so much to see and do in the eastern states. Life was an adventure both on and off campus.

Our first son, Caleb Livingstone, was born one cold morning in January 2003 in Hershey, Pennsylvania, home of the great chocolate bar. We teased that he was our "Chocolate Baby." Caleb brought immense joy. Jacob and I were instantly smitten and took up the parental role with great enthusiasm. We proudly watched as Caleb smiled his first smile, took his first step, said his first word, and cut his first tooth. He couldn't have been more perfect for our family.

Soon after Caleb turned one, we felt it was time to return to Idaho. Our time at Mount Zion had made a huge impact on our lives, and we were grateful for all we had experienced. But as all seasons in life eventually come to an end, so did this one. We knew it was time for the next chapter.

Jacob had it all figured out. Instead of renting a U-Haul, he traded in our car and bought a truck and trailer, planning that when we reached Idaho, we'd sell the trailer and trade the truck for a family vehicle. Somehow this made complete sense to my husband.

We put his plan into action. We packed up our few belongings and loaded them into the new trailer. Our departure was bittersweet. So many beautiful memories and friendships had been made there that it was hard to say good-bye. Transitions can be difficult, but we were confident in God's leading and guiding us as He always had. There was no need to worry.

It wasn't easy starting over. Jacob's parents kindly allowed us to live with them until we could afford our own place. By this time, baby number two was on the way. We prayed and asked God to give us our own home before the baby came. Only weeks before our second son's birth, we became proud homeowners. It was simple small starter home, but it was ours, and we were thrilled. We spent hours painting and cleaning, and within a couple weeks, our new home was ready.

Clayton Jeremiah joined our family in December 2004. It was definitely more of a challenge this time around, as there were no more leisurely naps for momma every time the baby slept because now I had a toddler to keep up with. But that didn't dim the joy another baby brought to our family. Clayton was just as delicious as his big brother was as a baby. We were very proud of our two tiny young men. God had truly blessed our family.

We spent several years in our small two-bedroom, two-bath home, which was perfect for us, and we loved it. When we moved in, the backyard hadn't been completed, so finishing it was the first large project we tackled, but it certainly wasn't the last. Over the course of our time in that house, Jacob built a covered back patio, painted the exterior of the house, and had new carpet installed.

Eventually, we found a wonderful church, began making friends, and soon felt right at home. Jacob and I volunteered in the nursery and taught children's church. Jacob joined the men's events, and I began attending the women's Bible studies. It was good to be a part of this special church family.

Jacob and I felt that one day God would call us into full-time ministry. We didn't know where, when, or what, but our heart's desire was to serve Him wherever He directed. Jacob hoped that one day we'd go abroad as missionaries. Before we were married, he had gone on several mission trips. He loved sharing God's love by meeting people's physical needs, which was often through construction work. Jacob was a gifted craftsman.

But for now, we were content with this season. After all, one can and should serve Jesus each day of his or her life whether in full time ministry or not. Every day is an opportunity to glorify our Savior, Jesus Christ.

Soon our family welcomed another member into its midst. Our first daughter, Lacey Camille, was born in May 2006. How exciting it was to have a girl! She was Daddy's little princess for sure. Finally seeing a bit of pink in the washing machine after so many loads of blue was a thrill!

If there was even the slightest dull moment before Lacey's arrival, there certainly wasn't now. Our days were all action from morning till night and any extra time in between. I was a full-time mom and loved it. Although certainly not easy, it was worth the effort. There were plenty of hard days when simply taking a shower felt like a vacation and many long nights when babies cried and sick toddlers threw up. But I wouldn't have traded it for anything. In those moments when tiny arms hug your neck and pudgy lips kiss your cheek, you don't want anything else.

Jacob worked full time during the day and each evening put on his "Super Daddy" cape and spent time with his children. The moment he walked in the door, the kids scurried off to hide. Usually soft giggles gave away their hiding spots, but Jacob pretended not to notice. He'd sneak up on them with a great big "Boo!" which started a chorus of screams and laughter as they fled from hiding. Daddy then caught them in his arms and ran around. Finally, everyone ended up in a dog pile on the living room floor.

Truly, those were the golden years. I'm not implying that life was perfect. We had our fair share of issues and inconveniences as everyone else does, but we also had so much to be thankful for. We had good health, a warm house, food, three adorable children, and love—true love—that held us all together.

7

Beginnings and Endings

We quickly outgrew our small home. Caleb and Clayton shared a room with bunk beds. Our room had a very large master closet that worked nicely as the baby suite. However, Lacey had outgrown her crib, was now in a toddler bed, and would soon need a normal bedroom. We were emotionally attached to our house but realized it was time for a larger one.

We put our house on the market and began searching for a new one. Looking out our kitchen window and seeing a "for sale" sign blowing in the breeze brought mixed feelings—sorrow over having to part from what we had grown to love and yet excitement for what we hoped we would learn to love.

House hunting is thrilling at first but can be exhausting when you can't find what you're looking for and have little ones to get in and out of the car. House after house came and went, and still we hadn't found the right one. Friends of ours were building a house, so we decided to look into that for ourselves. We found it to be a good deal, so with great enthusiasm, we chose this route.

Meanwhile, our home sold, and we needed to be out soon. While our new house was under construction, we rented a duplex. We packed up everything and moved into a temporary house. Walking through our empty home for the last time, leaving the keys on the counter, and closing the door was an emotional moment. I could almost smell the cookies baking in the oven at Christmas and hear the laughter at the kids' birthday parties. The memories begged us not to leave, but once again, it was a new season for our family. It was time to go.

Our new home was built over the course of the spring and summer 2008. We often stopped by the jobsite to see what changes had been made since our last visit. Jacob was familiar with new home construction and enjoyed inspecting the work. The workers couldn't pull the wool over this homeowner's eyes, not that they were trying to. But in case they did, Jacob would know.

I look back on that summer and thank the Lord for all the fun times and "sunshiny days" we shared as a family, for unbeknownst to us, they wouldn't last much longer. Storm clouds were forming on the horizon of our lives, and in only a matter of months, our world would come crashing down. Aren't you glad Jesus keeps knowledge of the future from us? If He didn't, we would spend more time fretting over what is to come than living the present day to the fullest.

We took several weekend getaways as a family. Acquaintances graciously allowed us the use of their float house. What a delight being on the water! We woke up to the warm summer sun each day and ate breakfast on the deck. The kids had a blast splashing in the water or riding the paddleboat. A friend of ours brought his jet ski over and took us for rides. I was afraid my little ones might fly off, but Randy took good care of them, and they were just fine. We all had a blast.

Caleb, Clayton, and Lacey loved hanging out on the bridge that led from the house to the shore. Their greatest pastime there was finding rocks on the beach, taking them up to the bridge, and then launching them over the edge—the bigger the rock, the bigger the splash, the bigger the smile. On a few occasions, Jacob was on the bridge holding one end of a long rope. The other end was attached to a small inflatable boat in which sat the three kids.

They whooped and hollered as Jacob gave a tug on the boat and sent it sailing under the bridge. When it drifted out as far as the rope would reach, Jacob would tug it back, and under the bridge it went. They could have done this for hours. Children never seem to tire of simple fun.

Our family didn't necessarily have to go anywhere for a good time. Memories were made right outside the front door. The kids and I would often be on the front lawn when Jacob returned home from work. He'd pulled his truck into the driveway, cut the engine, and greet everyone with hugs and kisses as the kids chimed in together, "Spray us with the hose, Daddy!"

Jacob and I would then climb into the back of the pickup, dangle our legs over the side, and discuss the day's events as he held the hose, showering the kids with water. The nozzle gave him the ability to control the flow of water with perfect accuracy. Sometimes he narrowed in on a specific child; other times, he encompassed them all. Screams of delight filled the summer air as the kids ran in circles, dancing and laughing together.

Summer was nearing an end, and our new home was finally complete. Jacob and I made the last walk through with our realtor, who wanted to be sure everything was finished to our satisfaction. We were thrilled as we inspected each room. This beautiful brand-new house was ours. It was really true! We signed the final papers and were given the keys.

We packed our belongings and loaded them into a U-Haul. With the help of friends and family members, we were out of the rental and into our new home within a few days. The kids ran from room to room, exploring their new territory. Lacey finally had a bedroom! The boys still shared a room, but it was large and spacious.

I was excited about the master closet, which was large enough to be used for clothing *and* an office. The house even had an extra room that we decided to use as toy/guest room. Wow! Such luxury! And three bathrooms too! We felt extremely blessed as we began making ourselves at home in our new dwelling.

What we thought was a beginning was in fact an ending. Without knowing it, we had just closed the last normal chapter of our lives. A new chapter was about to begin, a terrifying, painful one. We didn't realize what the future held for us, but if asked, I know we would have confidently said, "No matter what, we will trust Jesus because He holds our world in His hands."

8

What's This?

"Jacob, what's this?" I pointed to a mole on his back.

"What?" He had just finished his shower and was getting ready for the day.

"It's a mole," I continued. "But it looks different from your other ones."

Jacob paused a moment, looked in the mirror, and briefly surveyed the dark spot. "It's probably nothing to worry about." Soon he was dressed, and the conversation changed to a different subject. But I felt uneasy. I couldn't shake the gnawing thought that that mole didn't look right.

Days passed. Every time Jacob removed his shirt, there was that mole. Where had it come from anyway? I didn't remember noticing it before. It seemed to appear all of a sudden out of nowhere. How had it grown so large without previous detection? Jacob continued denying it was anything significant.

But I kept hearing my mother's words ringing in my ears, cautioning me on the seriousness of a mole that suddenly changed in appearance. So I decided to call and run it past her. When I explained what it looked like and how large it was, she said, "Oh, Dawn, that doesn't sound good." My stomach churned with worry, but I tried pushing it aside. No way could it be cancer. Certainly this would blow over and be all right.

However, when the mole began bleeding, I could no longer ignore the prompting in my heart. Inwardly, I knew something was wrong.

"Honey, we need to have this looked at, especially now that it's bleeding," I told Jacob, and he consented.

Jacob went alone to his appointment with the dermatologist, which was during his work hours. I was at home with the children and honestly wasn't feeling up to par. We recently found out the happy news that baby number four was on its way, and morning sickness had set in. Thankfully, I was through the worst of it and was on my way to recovery. However, I was weak after a month of nausea and vomiting.

Jacob came home that night and recounted the events of his appointment. The doctor chatted a bit and then got right to business. After examining the mole, he sliced it off to send to the lab. He put a bandage over the area and told Jacob the results would be in within the next couple days.

That was pretty much the extent of the appointment. We were left wondering as we waited to hear more. But a cloud of uneasiness hung in the air. The subject was dropped for the night, but the agitation in my heart wouldn't subside. This constant companion whispered, "What if? What if?" I didn't want to think about "what if." I wanted everything to be all right. It had to be.

We didn't have to wait long. The next day, Jacob received a call. The lab results were in, and the dermatologist wanted to go over them with Jacob in person. Jacob called me from work to let me know he would swing by the doctor's office before he came home. He didn't tell me that the doctor had advised him to bring me along for the appointment. Jacob realized this was not a good sign. Knowing how badly I felt, he didn't want to make it any worse for me than it was about to be. He would face it alone.

That night our world shattered into a million pieces. "It's malignant melanoma," Jacob soberly told me.

"What does that mean?" I asked.

"I'm not completely sure," he continued, "except the doctor made it sound very serious. He sent me home with some pamphlets and referred me to a surgeon in Spokane." The dermatologist had not been able to tell him how far it had spread. He just knew Jacob had it.

I could barely believe it. My husband had cancer? Certainly this was only a bad dream. I needed to wake up so it would instantly vanish. But it was not a nightmare. It was true, all of it. What was going to happen? There were still so many unknowns. Fear was knocking at the door, inviting itself in. If the invitation was denied, it tried the windows. At any available opportunity, it whispered its icy thoughts in our ears.

What lay in store for us? I felt like we were standing at the entrance of a large cave. The journey through the tunnel looked dark. Was that rolling thunder? Perhaps it would soon lead to the sun again. But what if it didn't? What if the tunnel was long with no end in sight? What if there was great sorrow? I couldn't think about that. I wouldn't. However, no matter what happened, Jacob and I believed that God was in control and would walk through this with us. We would trust Him and believe for complete healing.

9

The Beginning of Sorrow

Jacob was scheduled for surgery to remove the rest of the cancer around the original mole site. This was a big deal. Jacob had never undergone surgery before. In fact, neither one of us had ever spent much time in a hospital. However, that was about to change. Soon those long halls and the smell of latex gloves would become all too familiar.

The first surgery left Jacob with a massively long scar on his back, as they had dug deep and wide to remove as much cancerous tissue as they could. They determined that Jacob not only had malignant melanoma, but he also had the most aggressive form. Some melanomas are more superficial and lay flush on the skin. These don't spread as deeply or as quickly. However, Jacob had the nodular kind, the form that appears as a raised lump and quickly penetrates deeply into the layers of tissue. With this diagnosis, it was extremely probable that the cancer had already become invasive. Therefore, they strongly recommended that Jacob undergo further biopsies to determine if and how far it had spread.

Fortunately, my morning sickness was over, so I was able to support Jacob through each test and surgery. However, the joy of this pregnancy had vanished, like it didn't even exist, for our minds were so consumed with Jacob's health and what the next step would be. Our baby was quietly tucked away for now. There was plenty on our plate as it was. We prayed and believed life would be more stable by the time our little one came. Jacob often said that he knew God must have a plan for this baby because we certainly wouldn't have tried to have a baby at a time like this. Jesus was completing our family with this child. Although it seemed like an insane time, Jesus always works right on schedule. He would provide me with the needed grace and strength to carry this vibrant gift of life at a time when its daddy's life was fading.

Christmas was near, but there wasn't much room in our hearts for celebrating. This cancer thing had put a huge damper on life. We trudged on. Jacob continued undergoing tests, scans, and biopsy surgery. Finally, his surgeon determined the verdict and asked us to meet with him.

We sat in the examination room of the cancer center, waiting for the doctor to enter. My stomach was in knots as usual. I hated each and every meeting we had with the surgeon and felt like a small child ready to scream and run from the room. I wished it were acceptable for grown women to behave that way. But since it was not, I remained in my chair. I loved my husband more than any other person on Earth. How could he, my man, have cancer? This couldn't be happening! But it was. All too soon, we heard approaching footsteps, and the door opened.

Jacob's surgeon sat down before us. He always tried being pleasant, but I noticed he never smiled. How could he, with a job like his? I'm sure he knew deep inside that most of the people he saw in his office and on the operating table would not live long.

The doctor began explaining the results of the biopsies. Since cancer had been found in the lymphatic system, Jacob was considered stage three malignant melanoma of the nodular type. I was too afraid to ask what that meant and how many stages there were, but I quickly perceived it wasn't a good thing. He continued explaining his other concerns and then gave his treatment advice, but my brain had already shut down. I couldn't handle any more bad news. I was about to lose it. It was all I could do to hold back the tears until the meeting was over.

Finally, the doctor was finished. We walked out to our car. The night was dark and the air cold; the frigid temperature penetrated every fiber of my body. The darkness was blacker than usual. Jacob and I walked in silence until we reached the car and climbed in. At last, we were alone.

I completely broke down. The tears fell uncontrollably, as sorrow and fear gripped my heart. They were strangling me and wouldn't let go. Our world was crashing in all around us, and there was nothing we could do to stop it.

As Jacob drove, he held his composure as was typical of him. I, on the other hand, was a pregnant, emotional wreck and cried and cried. We had planned to do a bit of Christmas shopping after this appointment. While the kids were being taken care of, we thought we'd make a mini date out of it. Shopping was the last thing I wanted to do at a time like this, but Jacob was insistent. He was so brave and strong and knew I needed to keep going. As he pulled into the parking spot, I sobbed to him how much I loved him.

"I know," he sweetly said.

We stepped out of the car and walked into the store.

10

The Grim Reality (2008–2009)

Christmas came and went that year without much fanfare. We tried to make it special for the kids, but our hearts were not in it. Jacob was on a strict diet that pretty much eliminated all the fun food people love to eat during the holidays. He was a good soldier, though, and had a great attitude. I admired his calm courage. He not only faced the mental challenges that come when a person is diagnosed with a killer disease, but also the physical discomfort that accompanies multiple biopsies.

Jacob's surgeon recommended an axillary lymph node dissection as the next plan of attack. Since the lymph node biopsy under his right arm had come back positive, it was highly probable that more nodes had been infected. Therefore, it was best to completely remove the rest of the lymphatic system in that area. The surgeon explained there would be lasting effects from such a surgery. Jacob didn't take this lightly. With a great amount of thought, prayer, and discussion, we decided to proceed with surgery. After the surgery was scheduled, all we could do was wait and pray that the lab results would come back negative and that no more cancer would be found.

As we waited, life continued. The sun rose and set. Caleb turned six. For his birthday, we took the family to a local ski resort whose hotel had an indoor water park and was offering a package deal. We knew the kids would have a blast in the water, and Jacob wanted to teach the boys how to ski. That trip became one of the highlights of that year for our family, a moment in time when we almost forgot the trial at hand. Almost … not completely.

Clayton also had a birthday. He turned four. For his birthday, we invited a bunch of his little friends to come over and make ginger-bread houses. If you have any imagination at all, I am sure you can picture what this event looked like with kids, candy, and frosting. It was a special time, though, with friends and family chatting and laughing—another one of those rare moments when life seemed as it used to be.

Our boys were vibrant and full of life. They lived for the times when Daddy came home from work and played with them. But these occasions were becoming fewer and farther between, as Jacob eventually was not able to wrestle and tumble as he used to. He barely had time to heal from one surgery before it was time for the next one. This put a damper on things for Caleb and Clayton; however, they still managed to get their energy out one way or another.

Our little princess, Lacey, was two. Her mannerisms were sweet and genteel, although she could hold her ground when needed. She loved pink, purple, and anything that sparkled! However, she was not afraid to plod around in the mud right beside her big brothers. We were hoping this next baby would be a girl. My dream in particular was that Lacey would have a little sister to keep her company. Before I became pregnant, Lacey and I prayed every night for Jesus to give her a baby sister. Now that a baby was on the way, we hoped that God would answer with a "she."

The day of Jacob's surgery finally arrived. We left the kids in good hands and headed for the hospital. We knew this surgery was more involved than the others but were confident that Jesus was with us and would guide the surgeon's hands. Throughout this entire battle, we felt our faith being challenged. Would we give in and flounder in grief and despair, or would we stand strong on the Word of God and trust Him completely? Isaiah 43:1–3 says:

...Fear not: for I have redeemed thee, I have called thee by thy name; thou art mine. When thou passest through the waters, I will be with thee; and through the rivers, they shall not overflow thee: when though walkest through the fire thou shalt not be burned; neither shall the flame kindle upon thee. For I am the Lord thy God, the Holy One of Israel, thy Saviour:...

After arriving at the hospital, Jacob was taken to pre-op. I was able to remain with him until the anesthesiologist was ready. It had become somewhat normal seeing him in a hospital gown and yet still so foreign. I didn't like it. Jacob didn't belong in a hospital bed, preparing for surgery. But nonetheless, he was.

When the time came, I left him and took my seat in the waiting room. How familiar it had become. I prepared for the long wait. The clock slowly ticked, minute by minute. Hours passed, and I grew restless. This surgery was taking much longer than the others. When would it be over? Was everything okay?

Finally, Jacob's surgeon appeared around the corner, still in his scrubs. He sat down next to me and explained the surgery and how it went. He was able to remove the lymph tissue to his satisfaction and had sent it off to the lab. The official results would be available in a few days, however ...

My heart pounded. I didn't know if I wanted to hear his next words. *Please tell me you didn't find any more cancer*, I thought to myself.

The surgeon then told me that, yes, he had found more melanoma in Jacob's lymph nodes. He was sure by their appearance that they were cancerous.

I don't remember much of what he said after that. Then he was gone, and I was left alone to collect my thoughts and emotions. My heart wept. Jacob, now in recovery, was just coming out of the anesthesia and wasn't aware of anything the doctor had just told me. I knew how much he had been counting on a clear report. How could I tell him?

Time continued to pass, and still no word from the nurses' station. I grew lonely and afraid. It's amazing how Jesus works in the times we need Him the most. He often sends someone to us to be His arms extended. In one of my hardest moments, our pastor appeared. Seeing a familiar face was wonderful after spending the day alone in the waiting room. He sat with me, and we talked. When I told him about the surgeon's report, he offered words of strength and support. I was thankful for the presence of a dear friend in a time when I needed it so desperately.

At long last, I was notified that Jacob was in a room, and I could go to him. Pastor Dan and I made our way down the hall and up the elevator to his room. When I entered, my stomach sank. Jacob was in a lot of pain and could barely move. He looked so fragile as the nurse tended to him. Jacob softly greeted Dan, and they chatted for a few moments as the nurse explained to me how to care for Jacob once he went home.

Soon the nurse left us alone in the room. I went to my husband and stood by his bed. I took his hand in mine, letting him know I was there, but my heart was breaking inside. I knew the moment was at hand. Jacob would want to know.

"Dawn," he whispered. "Did they find any more cancer?" His eyes searched mine, looking for hope.

How could I say the words? How could I tell him? "Honey," I said with all the strength I could muster. "The surgeon said they did find more cancer."

It was as if I had stabbed my own darling in the chest. A wave of sorrow and disappointment swept over his face. Now that so much cancer was in his lymph system, who knew where else it had already spread? As I held Jacob's hand, we both knew that our love and the love of Jesus would hold us through the duration of this storm. But it still hurt deep down in our souls.

11

We Walk by Faith

Within a couple days, Jacob came home to begin the long recovery process. I was his nurse and constant companion. I carefully followed the nurse's instructions, and little by little, the wound began to heal. Unfortunately, though, that didn't mean the cancer inside his body was gone.

As Jacob grew stronger, we needed to decide the next plan of attack, which was not an easy decision. We had a lot of advice dished out to us by well-meaning doctors, friends, and family. But ultimately we needed to know what God wanted us to do.

With faith in Jesus, we stepped forward in the direction we felt He was leading. We knew deep inside that Jesus held healing in His almighty hands. Any and all healing would come through Him and would be to His honor and glory. I watched my beautiful Jacob hold to this the entire battle. He never lost sight of or let His confidence drift from Jesus to the power of man. Yes, it's true that God can work through treatments to bring healing. Yes, it's true that sometimes they are effective and sometimes they aren't. But ultimately, behind it all, who is it that holds all things in His hands? Who is it that decides whether a treatment will be successful or not? It's God. Our times and seasons are in *His* hands. He is in complete control.

The treatment we chose was out of state. Jacob cleared everything with his boss, and we packed up our kids and headed south. Just before our departure, Jacob discovered another lump under the skin, and we knew what that meant. So with heavy hearts, we made our way on the next step of the journey that lay before us. We didn't know what was ahead, but we knew the One who did. And that's all that mattered.

For the next month and a half, Jacob was in treatment. The children were able to be with us for the first half. This time was more bitter than sweet, but I treasure the moments we were able to share together as a family. It was as if the Lord was allowing something special for our family during our last days with Jacob. We were in Southern California and Mexico, so the setting certainly inspired a vacation-like presence. And for the children it was a vacation. However, for Jacob and me, it wasn't completely so, as we felt the inner throb and the nagging dread. We knew Jesus was with us, but it was still hard and very scary at times to walk by faith. If we took our eyes off Jesus even for a moment, we were doomed to sink.

We could relate to the apostle Peter as he walked on the raging sea to meet the Lord. As long as Peter kept his eyes focused on the face of Christ, his feet stayed firm. But when he grew distracted by the fearsome waves and the howling wind, he began to sink. When he cried out, Jesus was right there to lift him up. He didn't let Peter sink to the bottom of the sea. The same Jesus who held Peter's hand was holding our hands too. No matter how scared and downcast we became, Jesus was there to pick us up and help us carry on. His master plan was in progress, and He knew we needed His strength and courage to fulfill it.

During our trip, my mother came to stay with us and tend to the children. Jacob required a lot of rest. Since our accommodations were tight, I needed help keeping the kids busy yet quiet. Caleb was able to continue with his schooling, which kept him occupied, and Clayton and Lacey often joined him with their preschool workbooks as well. Frequently, my mom and I took the children outside to play. Caleb and I kicked a soccer ball around while mom held tea parties with Clayton and Lacey. With the kids outside, Jacob was better able to rest.

The happiest times were Jacob's days off from treatment when we could go do something fun. Getting away from the treatment center and staying with our friends, Jim and Audrey, in their gorgeous condo was wonderful. What a treat that was.

Jacob's work had given us tickets to the San Diego Zoo and Sea World. We felt so blessed. The zoo held much excitement for the children, but it involved a lot of walking. Normally, the children's little legs would have been the concern, but not now. Jacob was the one I was worried about. Throughout the day, I pushed the stroller for him because I could tell he was weary. There I was, big belly and all, huffing and puffing up and down the hills. Jacob needed me to be strong for him, but after awhile, he would insist it was his turn again.

I wasn't used to seeing him tire so quickly. He'd always been strong and hardly ever got sick, and his weakness scared me. When he finally found a place to rest, I kept a distant but watchful eye on him.

Sea World was the next adventure. It was fun yet, once again, exhausting for Jacob. He went on a few rides with the kids, stood in long lines in the sun, and did a lot of walking. The highlights of the day were the sea life shows with the jumping seals, whales, and dolphins, which thrilled the children. During one of these performances, a deep sense of grief and fear washed over me, as I watched the family sitting in front of us. When I narrowed in on the father and his children, my tears welled up and spilled over. I was thankful I could hide behind the sunglasses I was wearing. No one could see my tears, but they were there.

Will my children have their daddy with them much longer? I could barely believe I was thinking these thoughts. And yet I was. This *was* happening to us! My husband had a deadly form of cancer. This was reality ... but how could it be? Oh, my dear Jesus, how could this be?

Near the end of Jacob's treatment plan, we had to face that it was not accomplishing what we prayed it would. The tumors were not stopping but were growing. Now what to do? After much prayer, we decided Jacob would transfer to another treatment center that came highly recommended and happened to be in the same general area. The only drawback was it wouldn't allow children to remain on a permanent basis. We quickly arranged a way to transport our precious little ones back home. My brother, Josiah, and his wife, Valoree, would fly down and drive the kids and our car back home. This seemed like a perfect plan.

While I was busy getting everything ready for the kids to go home, Jacob was admitted into his new treatment center. I remained with the children and Sarah, a special friend of mine who graciously flew down to help in any way she could. She was a great support for me as I prepared for the children's departure. I felt the weight of the world on my shoulders as I carefully made sure our bills back home were paid and the kids were packed. There were a million things to remember to do. I also had to postpone scheduled prenatal visits back home, as this pregnancy was just not at the top of the list right now. Since this was my fourth baby, I wasn't concerned if I missed a few visits. I knew the routine.

My mind and heart were under tremendous pressure. It's amazing how the grace and strength of Jesus is right there to hold us up when we are in dire need. "He giveth power to the faint; and to them that have no might He increaseth strength" (Isaiah 40:29). My strength had long since run out, and now I was being powered from above. When our lives are activated with this kind of power, we are equipped with all we need to accomplish whatever lies ahead.

Finally, everything was packed, and all was ready for the children's departure. Josiah and Valoree arrived, and the very next day, they took me to be with Jacob at his treatment center. We had to say good-bye to our children. I felt deep sadness as I kissed their little faces and hugged each one, for I knew it might be awhile before I would see them again. They were traveling so far, and I wanted them to reach home safely. I wanted them to mind their manners and be obedient. A mother's heart yearns for all to be well.

I tried to smile and be brave for the children, but inside, I wanted to burst into tears and cling to them and not let them go. We took a family picture, commemorating the day. The camera captured our last family photo. Our unborn child would never make it to Daddy's lap in a family photo shoot. Once again, I am grateful that the Lord kept the future hidden that day. Had I known, I couldn't have smiled.

Jacob and I spent the next month together. We were each other's constant companion and would have had it no other way. I look back on this time and am so grateful for it. The Lord knew we needed a respite, for the fiercest fury was yet to come. Not being on constant alert with the needs of the children was strange. It was so quiet and peaceful. My heart soon calmed regarding our separation from the kids, and I was able to completely soak in this time alone with my husband. He and I read the Bible, took walks on the beach, played games, and watched movies together. We snuggled and were able to laugh and smile as we enjoyed one another's presence in spite of the deep dread of what lay ahead.

Jacob spent his last birthday in this life with me. Number twenty-nine. The staff did their best to make it special for him. It was simple but sweet. I wish the kids could have been with us on that day, but they were hundreds of miles away with my parents.

Another "last" was the photo taken of Jacob and me on the beach. Our dear friend and pastor had flown down to see us for a couple days, so we took him to see a few sights, one of them being the beach at sunset. In the photo, the beautiful ocean with the soft tones of the setting sun is in the background. My arms are around Jacob, and my head is resting against his, and we are both smiling. I didn't like this photo of us for a long time after Jacob's death, but I cherish it now. However, on our faces and in our eyes there is a tiredness and lack of sparkle—a sadness. But still, I am thankful to Jesus that He gave us this one last photo shoot. Jesus is so wonderful like that.

12

Fading Fast

Finally! It was time to return home. We'd been gone a long time and were more than ready to get back. Little did we know as we stepped off the plane the intensity of the battle that was still to come.

I was trained to administer Jacob's treatment from home and would soon find out what "tired to the bone" really means. But with Jesus by my side, I was able to keep putting one foot in front of the other. My trust was in God, knowing that in this life there will be hardships and trials (John 16:33). Some will be as great as tidal waves and others might be messy puddles. The fires will burn hot with the flames of testing, crackling. But through them all, we have the promise from God that He will not leave us alone. He will walk by our side constantly (Isaiah 43:2). Not even for a split second will he turn His back on us (Matthew 28:20). We may feel abandoned as sorrow threatens to drown us or burn us to ashes. But Jesus is right there, holding out His strong hand and keeping us safe. Every moment of every day, Jesus is constantly watching over His children.

Jacob's work flew us home—and first class, at that. What a treat! We arrived late in the evening and were greeted at the airport by Jacob's parents, Fred and Leslie. Josiah and Valoree were at our house and greeted us when we arrived. What a surprise awaited us. People from my brother's church had come together and finished our fence. Now our children could safely play outside while I was busy indoors. We were delighted beyond words. Valoree and a group of ladies cleaned our house, and friends from our church put flowers on the counter and food in the refrigerator. We felt loved and welcomed before we even put a foot in the door.

Jacob and I were happy to be home and yet overwhelmed by so many new adjustments. I immediately set to work figuring out Jacob's new treatment plan, which required an immense amount of preparation and diligence. A strict schedule was necessary in order to stay on top of all it required. There was no way I would be able to do it alone. I was seven months pregnant and had three little ones still to care for.

I am so thankful for the friends and family members who came to my rescue. Jacob's parents moved down the street in order to be available whenever a need arose. My mother, Beth, drove from Montana as much as she could. Josiah and Valoree were only the next town away and countless friends from church pitched in to help in any way they could. We were surrounded by love and support. This was a battle we could not fight alone.

Jacob was able to resume work for a short time after returning home. But he was not the same. He lacked his former energy and vigor. He had always been a strong man who was able to handle just about anything that came his way. But all that was fading, and I watched him rapidly weaken. Seeing him weak and tired pained me.

One day, Jacob returned home especially frail in body and soul. He had gone to the hardware store and was exhausted when he walked through the doors. "Dawn, I could barely pick up my feet. All I could do was drag them across the floor. I looked over my shoulder and saw another young man. He walked with strength and speed. I used to be like that."

My heart broke. It was hard for Jacob to watch himself deteriorate, and soon he completely quit work. His body no longer sustained him throughout a full or even half a workday. My darling was fading, and it was happening too fast.

At times, Jacob grew discouraged. He didn't understand why the Lord was holding back His hand of healing. During these times of discouragement, I called our pastor and asked him to pray.

My moments of discouragement were much more frequent than Jacob's. I wept often but tried not to cry around him. Instead, I waited until I was alone, such as folding laundry or taking a shower. The tears would roll down my cheeks, and the pain and weariness was almost more than I could handle.

On one such occasion, I was alone in our bedroom. I fell to the floor and buried my head in the carpet. I cried to the Lord for deliverance from this great trial and storm that was shaking our lives. It hurt so much, and fear constantly tried forcing its way into my heart. Caleb found me as I was weeping and asked, "Mommy, why are you crying?"

"Because I want Jesus to heal Daddy," I replied.

"He will," Caleb said. His little heart held no fear. I too believed Jesus was able to heal Jacob, but the battle raged long and hard, and Jacob and I were weary. I didn't know how much more we could handle.

13

The Baby

The weaker Jacob became the less tolerant he was of noise. He was in a great deal of pain and needed the house to be quiet. He wasn't his usual self anymore, and it was hard on everyone—even him.

As you can imagine, it became an issue having the children around during the day. I tried the best I could to keep them quiet, but even their happy laughter and the normal pitter-patter of little feet throughout the house began wearing on Jacob, and he grew irritable. It often became extremely tense around our home.

On one occasion, Jacob sharply reprimanded Lacey for some small offense. I took her into the bathroom to talk things over. As I held her in my arms, my heart broke again. I buried my face in her hair and began to weep. What was happening to our family? Jacob and I were both worn out. I was constantly on the go from morning till evening, and Jacob was just as worn out from being sick. He didn't mean to be cross; I knew it wasn't really who he was. The battle raged furiously hot. We two soldiers were growing weary yet still refused to give up.

Finally, I knew something must be done with the children. There were a number of friends who wanted to watch the kids one day a week. Soon, someone covered each weekday, and the children were cared for from morning till afternoon. But I kept them home on the weekends. Our family was being tightly stretched and was wearing thin. I knew the kids were in good hands, but being juggled around was still difficult on them. They seemed oblivious to it, but Jacob and I could tell. Their attitudes and manners were slipping. We tried the best we could, but for the present, our main focus was on Daddy getting better. The rest would have to wait.

By now Jacob was completely housebound. He never left home unless it was for a doctor's appointment. The battle raged on and on. I'd look out the window at the world and in my heart, scream in silent agony. I felt like Jacob and I were prisoners in our own home. I longed to be free. I missed our old life and craved for it back again. I wanted Jacob to be healthy and strong like he used to be.

I watched in anguish as day by day Jacob's body grew weaker. My once robust man was now feeble and could barely walk from the bed to the chair. Once he reached his destination, he would sit down, panting. Even a short distance was almost too much for him. His face was pale, all natural color gone. Even his hair was different and lacked its healthy sheen. It shocked me to see him actually take on the appearance of an old man. On several occasions, he went to the emergency room for a blood transfusion, which always perked him up temporarily. But it never lasted more than a couple of weeks. Jacob tried a couple other treatment plans that had been advised, but to no avail. He grew increasingly worse.

Each day, Jacob's body continued to fade, but our unborn child continued to thrive. As my due date quickly approached, our hearts cried out, "Jesus, please heal Jacob before the baby comes … please, before the baby comes … please, Jesus, please!" Day after day came and went, bringing my due date closer and Jacob sicker. But we knew that Jesus would not give us anything too hard for us to bear, and that He had a purpose.

June 18 dawned, and I felt contractions on and off throughout the day. I tried ignoring them, hoping they were just rumblings that said the time was near but not immediate. However, by that evening, I knew that was not the case. I remember so clearly the sadness of that night. The birth of a child should bring joy, but on that night, Jacob and I cried together. He sat on the edge of the bed, and I knelt on the floor as the tears rolled. What was about to happen? How could we take care of a baby? And then Jacob, my wise man, prayed. He prayed for God's strength and help, for we were in desperate need. We needed Him to be strong in us. After a few moments, we arose and continued on with what lay ahead. If God was allowing this, He would provide the grace and strength we needed to see it through.

We chose to have our baby at home as we had done in the past. I asked Valoree to be with me and assist since Jacob didn't have the strength. She was more than willing. My midwife arrived and soon had me as comfortable as possible. Jacob put on instrumental worship music, which was lovely for everyone in the room and a soothing respite in spite of the pain at hand.

Our beautiful baby girl was born only a few hours later. I was filled with joy when I heard it was a girl. Jacob had a big smile too. Now he had two little princesses. Our prayers had been answered. Thank you, Jesus. At times, God answers our prayers exactly as we have asked. Other times, He answers in ways we can't fully understand. But with every prayer, He answers in the way He sees best, for it fits perfectly into His master plan for our lives and how our character is built. We either respond to His choice with an open heart or a closed one. He can do so much with a heart that trusts His wisdom over its own desire. In this, He is glorified.

Someone picked up the camera that night and took a few shots of Jacob and baby Lydia. In one precious photo, Jacob and our daughter are looking into each other's eyes. I wonder what thoughts were going through his mind as he gazed at his little girl. What silent prayer was he praying? I am sure he was wondering how long he had left to be with her and to enjoy her sweetness. The time was short, but I am thankful that God gave him those last precious months. Lydia had made it in time to see her daddy before they would have to wait till heaven to see one another again.

I rested for a couple days and then was back at it full steam ahead, baby and all. What I didn't think I could possibly handle, Jesus gave me the strength and grace to accomplish.

He will never lead us to something without supplying what we will need to get through it. It doesn't mean that it will be easy or even pleasant, but He will be there. His strength will be beautified in our weakness. His power will rest upon us. For when we are weak, He is strong in us (1 Corinthians 12:9–10).

14

The Weight of the World

The Cole house was silent as everyone lay sleeping in his or her bed. I rolled over, opened one eye, and looked at the clock. Relief surged through every fiber of my weary body. It was still early ... I didn't have to get up yet. I could sleep for a couple more hours. My alarm would wake me plenty early, but for now, I could snuggle back under the covers and rest. As I drifted back off to sleep, I prayed for strength to face the morning by the time it arrived. As of now, I didn't think I wanted to handle another day of this vicious life. I asked Jesus to help me want to face it and to do it well. My husband needed me to be strong for him. He looked to me in so many ways. I had to be there for him 100 percent. But I was *so* exhausted.

"Jesus, Jesus ... please help me ... " I whispered, and I drifted back to sleep.

A few hours later, my alarm went off. When I opened my eyes, I felt strength rise up from deep within. I wish I had the ability to describe the incredible grace Jesus poured upon me, which He did day after day after day. Often, I felt too weary to even want to step out of bed, but by morning, when it was time for me to face it, His grace came and lifted me up.

I always carefully prepared myself each morning. I made sure to do my hair and makeup every single day whether I was just going to be around home or not. I knew it meant a lot to Jacob to see his wife looking her best for him. I think it made him feel hopeful when he saw me pretty and not Miss Frumpy-Dumpy. I made it a priority because I knew it brought him joy.

Oh, my ... the time. I needed to make breakfast and wake the kids. I left Jacob quietly sleeping and rushed downstairs to start the morning routine. I let the kids sleep a little longer while I prepared breakfast. Jacob's diet was always different from ours. Everything he ate was strictly organic and took forever to prepare because it all had to be made from scratch. Throughout the course of the day, my kitchen often filled to overflowing with dishes, pots, and pans.

This particular morning would be organic oatmeal as it was every morning. His diet was definitely not what one would rush to the head of the line for. It was rather boring and lacked the fun comfort foods we all enjoy so much. After eating oatmeal every day for a long while you become quite the connoisseur of that fine grain. Jacob was very particular on how it was prepared. Some mornings I got it right and others ... well, I didn't.

As the oatmeal cooked, I squeezed fresh juice. Jacob started every morning with orange and progressed throughout the day with fresh veggie drinks. They had to be freshly squeezed and consumed as quickly as possible. This required constant attention. Often Jacob's mother came to help me out. She was a godsend since there wasn't any way I could have done all that juicing alone.

As I worked in my kitchen, I often glanced at the windowsill where I kept Scripture cards as a constant reminder of God's faithfulness. I meditated on them throughout the day, savoring each one. God's Word was my constant source of strength.

Oh, the baby was crying! Rats. I had hoped she would sleep longer. I zipped up the stairs to fetch her before she bothered Jacob with her cries. Lydia was a good baby for the most part. She was content and smiled a lot.

What a sweet darling you are, I thought as I kissed her little face and carefully nestled her in the infant saucer. It was designed for a much larger baby, but I had to keep working, so I stuffed blankets around her to keep her stable. She was still so young.

I finished Jacob's breakfast and took it up to our room. I gently nudged him. He rarely slept well at night, making it difficult to wake up in the morning. I left the tray on the bed for him and moved on to waking the children. I herded their sleepy bodies downstairs to the breakfast table. Soon they would be out the door and on to their "home" for the day.

The children's noise was a constant issue. As much as I loved them, it was such a relief when they were out of the house for a while, and I was able to focus more on Jacob and taking care of his needs. I felt less uptight and afraid that each noise would bother him.

The day went into high gear as soon as the kids were gone. I helped Jacob shower, which was a long ordeal since he needed to move slowly or he'd wear himself out. Sometimes Lydia would begin to cry, and our sweet baby would have to cry it out. She was not hurting and would be fine. I would shut her door and hurry back to Jacob. He was always concerned about Lydia, but I assured him she would be fine.

After his shower, I had to dress the tumor on his chest, which bled a lot and regularly needed new bandages. In the middle of all this, I still continued providing the fresh juices he needed combined with a zillion pills and an injection that I learned to administer. I disliked having to poke my husband, but I had to anyway.

Some days Jacob went away for treatment if he was able to travel. I drove carefully, avoiding as many bumps and potholes as possible since they jolted his body and caused him pain. Lydia was too tiny to be sent off with her older siblings, so she always went with us. Once in a while, she would cry in her car seat, which always made for a stressful trip. It's amazing what the crying of a baby can do to someone who is gravely ill. Jacob would become extremely agitated. The treatment center coming into view was a welcome sight to both of us.

However, this particular day, Jacob stayed put and I treated him from home. I helped him to his chair and made him as comfortable as possible. I carried a walkie-talkie and left the other one on a table near him. This system was superb.

The day slipped by as I ran from one task to another, and before I knew it, the kids were due back any second, and I needed to start working on Jacob's dinner. Friends from church brought dinner for the kids and me on a regular basis. Knowing I didn't have to prepare two sets of dinners was such a blessing.

Tonight's meal was take-and-bake pizza. The kids were home by now and running around. I turned the oven on to preheat. After shooing the kids out side along with their chatter, I slid the pizza in the oven. Jacob's meal was coming along nicely. His veggies needed to be cooked at a low temperature, which was very time consuming, but at least they were more nutritious that way.

The kitchen was a wreck as usual by this time of the day. Lydia began fussing, so I picked her up. After having four kids, one becomes pretty good at multitasking. I continued with her on my hip. The timer rang; the pizza was done. As I opened the oven, the hot air hit my face, and I turned Lydia away to protect her from the heat. I reached in to carefully remove the pizza from the oven with one hand.

Before I knew what happened, the pizza slipped from my hand, flipped on its face, and landed on the oven door. I was hot, completely exhausted from the day, and now this! Our ruined dinner lay in a melted heap all over the oven door. I could contain myself no longer and burst into tears.

These are the times when Jesus reaches out to us. He saw my weariness and had already prepared help for me. My brother and his wife happened to come over that evening. First, they calmed me down and then cleaned the oven. Their help meant so much to me. Dinner worked itself out somehow that night. I don't really remember what the kids and I ate, but I'm thinking it may have been topless pizza.

During days like that, it was important for me to remember to keep my eyes fixed on Jesus, as my strength came from Him. Often I looked too much toward the end I wanted—Jacob's healing—and grew frustrated and impatient. But God's Word says in Isaiah 40:29–31:

> He giveth power to the faint; and to them that hath no might He increaseth strength. Even the youths shall faint and be

weary, and the young men shall utterly fall: But they that wait upon the LORD shall renew their strength; they shall mount up with wings as eagles; they shall run, and not be weary, and they shall walk, and not faint.

I needed to keep waiting upon the Lord, focusing on Him in the here and now and not so much on the "when" of Jacob's healing. God would take care of everything in His timing. As my eyes and heart stayed fixed on Him, He renewed my strength and filled me up again ... and again ... and again. Every morning when I opened my eyes to a new day, He was there to lead me through it. As I looked to Him, He gave me the strength of an eagle soaring high on the wings of the wind. And whether the pizza fell, the oatmeal turned out wrong, the kids played too loudly, or Lydia began to cry, Jesus was there for me every moment, covering me with His amazing grace.

15

True Love

The day had been grueling like all the others. I was exhausted as the setting sun slipped behind the hills and was gone. The kids had said their prayers and were fast asleep. The baby was quiet too, at least for the moment. A hushed silence fell over the house. Our bedroom light was still on as it always was until at least midnight. Jacob didn't sleep well during the night and spent a lot of time lying awake, staring into the silent darkness. He dreaded bedtime and put it off as long as possible, holding onto each day.

He had spent the evening in his chair watching TV, which was a great distraction for him and filled his mind with something fun. Cooking shows were among his favorites. How he could watch them prepare all kinds of delicious food (not on his diet) and not go crazy was beyond me.

"Honey," he softly called. "I'm ready now."

I was asleep on the bed next to his chair. I often couldn't keep my eyes open as I waited for him to go to bed. In fact, there were times when I was so sound asleep that he had to call me several times before I heard him.

I roused myself and went to his side to help him move from his chair to our bed. Since it was in the same room, the walk was not far.

However, even this little exertion left him winded. He lay on his back, trying to catch his breath. After he recovered, he silently lay there, watching me move about the room.

His body was still, which meant he wasn't in any discomfort. Often it was the complete opposite. During those times, he moaned and jerked as sudden waves of pain shot through his slender frame. He tried so hard to be brave, but I could see the intensity on his face as he winced in agony and every muscle in his body tightened. On those nights, I sat by his side to help ease his tension. Often I rubbed his legs and feet or softly stroked his face with my fingertips, helping his furrowed brows to relax. But his favorite was for me to run my fingers through his hair. This calmed him the best of all.

But this night was a good one. There was no anguish in his expression. His muscles were relaxed as he quietly lay there, waiting for me to assist him. Every night had its routine as I prepared him for bed. It varied from time to time, but the basics remained the same.

It always took awhile since Jacob's body was so frail and unable to move quickly. He needed assistance in everything. What once was a simple task was now a monumental undertaking. There were times when I tried to rush the process, but he was good at reminding me to slow down. In my hastiness, I often bumped him in all the wrong spots. He preferred me to be methodical with each movement as it helped him relax.

I came to his side. "Honey, are you ready?"

"Yes," he quietly replied.

I began to change his dressings. The tumors on his body needed daily care. As I silently set to work, careful with each movement, my mind wandered back to the first days of being in love with this man. How strong he had been then. His large, six-foot-two frame was my dream come true. From head to toe, Jacob was a perfect image of Prince Charming himself. I was the happiest girl alive when I found out he was in love with me ...

A gentle touch on my arm brought me back to reality. I was positioned over Jacob's chest, changing his dressing. He softly stroked my arm. When I looked into his eyes, he didn't have to speak. I could clearly read what his heart was saying.

"Dawn, thank you ... I love you."

I gave him a smile that said, "I love you too."

Again, I was lost in thought, back in time. Oh, those amazing blue eyes of his had made my heart skip a beat when he looked at me. We had the habit that whenever one of us walked into the room, we searched for the other until our eyes met. We didn't have to speak. We knew we were in love, a love that, though tested, would remain faithful and true. The man before me now had changed in appearance, but he was still the same man I had fallen in love with years ago.

I leaned over my husband and spoke softly, "Honey, everything about you has changed, but your eyes are still the same." I wanted Jacob to know that although his manly appearance had been altered, those eyes that had captured my heart were the same. Sure, they lacked the sparkle they once had, but they were still the beautiful blue eyes that belonged to the man I loved with all my heart.

Jacob began to cry and whispered, "Dawn, you have only become more beautiful."

As I sit here today thinking back on that time, I can only imagine the thoughts going through his mind. He was starting to say good-bye without even realizing it, and it broke his heart.

Truly, Jacob's love was one of a kind. What an honor to be loved like that from a man like him. Never for an instant during our eight years of marriage did I ever doubt his love and commitment to me. He was a "one of a kind" guy and my hero too as he bravely fought through each day of that horrifying disease. He wasn't perfect. He had bad days also. But overall he suffered with courage and honor. He fought for his life because he knew how much the children and I depended on him, and he wanted to be around for us. He took the leadership position God had given him very seriously, but as time went on, he learned to let go. Deep down, I think he knew he wouldn't be around much longer.

I finished preparing Jacob for bed, softly kissed him, and turned off the lights. Our love had flourished in the good times and was now being strengthened in the bad ones. Truly, our love would never die.

16

The Triumphant Entry

Time has a way of slipping between your fingers like sand on the seashore. What at first is a complete handful in your grasp soon slips away and is gone, and all you are left with is a few granules in your palm. Before long, even those are carried away by a silent breeze. Time can't be stopped or held onto. It ticks on and on ... and eventually passes.

Our time left with Jacob was like that. We tried holding onto it for as long as possible, but eventually, it ran out. He was ready to go. I didn't recognize it at the time because I didn't want to. My husband had fought a courageous battle, but this soldier was worn out. His time had come to go home to glory, and heaven's gate was opening for him. The time was near at hand.

October 9 dawned. As I cared for Jacob that day, I could tell something was very wrong. He was not himself; he acted odd and could barely communicate with me. He was having trouble with his vision and at one point called me in a panic because he could hardly talk and couldn't move his arms or his legs. Then he slipped into semiconsciousness. After that, he said nothing except "Jesus."

The hours crept by. Finally, the fog lifted, and Jacob was back again, fully coherent, but his behavior had shaken me. I told him a little of what had happened, avoiding details so as not to scare him.

One thing I made sure to tell him was that while in his semiconscious state, he only said, "Jesus."

"I did?" His quiet but enthusiastic reaction showed how happy he was that when nothing else made sense to him, Jesus still did.

His treatment specialist came that evening. After the treatment, Jacob settled down to sleep. The children were in bed. Caleb and Lydia were the only two children with us at the house, as Clayton and Lacey were in Montana with my parents where they had been for two weeks but were due back in the morning.

As usual, I prepared Jacob for bed; only tonight was a shorter version since he was far too weak to move from his chair. I made sure he was comfortable with a blanket pulled up to his chin. Then I knelt by the footrest and began rubbing his feet.

Suddenly, he became violently ill, vomiting again and again. Each episode shook his fragile body. After each episode, he was extremely thirsty and pleaded for water. This went on all night long. I prayed for his stomach to settle so he and I could rest. We were both exhausted.

At times, he became quiet, and I thought sleep had come, but as soon as my head hit the pillow, it started all over again. I hopped up and went to his side, my heart breaking. His weak skeleton of a body was wrenched with pain. He was restless and uncomfortable and frequently asked me to change the dressing around the tumor on his chest. He couldn't sleep, and I was constantly up and down, attending to his needs. Thankfully, the children slept soundly that night and didn't need anything. Eventually, I grabbed a blanket and pillow and slept on the floor next to Jacob's chair. I needed to be as close as possible.

Morning finally came, and night was behind us. Up to that point, that had been the most horrifying night I'd ever known, but nothing compared to what I would experience in a matter of hours.

On Saturday, October 10, the sun was peeking through the blinds. The battle of the night before had left its mark on us; saying we were fatigued would be an understatement. Jacob wanted to eat but nothing sounded good. He was restless and couldn't be satisfied.

I knelt down by his chair, rested my head on my arms, and sat there looking at him. Concerned, my eyes searched his. I can't put into words the agony I felt that day. I didn't understand what was happening and felt so helpless. My whole world was wrapped up in this man who I loved more than life itself, and there was nothing I could do to free him from this nightmare. It just kept going on and on.

Jacob took a deep breath, slowly let out a long sigh, and placed his hand over his chest.

My heart melted. I was so afraid. "Is anything wrong?" I asked.

Not wanting me to worry, he sweetly answered, "No." He then turned his head and looked deeply into my eyes. Slowly, a beautiful smile spread across his face, as if all the cherished memories of our past melted into one. All the joy, laughter, and love of a lifetime were wrapped up in his smile, the most beautiful one I had seen during his entire sickness. It was his last gift to me. Almost like he was trying to say good-bye but couldn't bring himself to actually speak the words because he knew it would pierce my heart.

Jacob's weary face was so precious and his smile full of pure devotion. I was the only woman he had ever loved, and now it was time to say good-bye. That smile was my last personal moment with him before he stepped into eternity.

About midmorning, Jacob's fidgeting stopped, and he slipped back into a semiconscious state. He seemed very peaceful and slept a lot. I tried to wake him but could not. Shaken once again by his odd behavior, I knew deep inside that something was terribly wrong.

During the early afternoon, my mom came back from Montana with Clayton and Lacey. As soon as they came in, I hugged them and said, "Let's go say hi to Daddy."

I quietly took them into his room, not knowing if he would be aware of their presence or not. No sooner had we walked in and stood by the arm of his chair that he opened his eyes and with a big smile quietly whispered, "Hi, Clayton. Hi, Lacey. I missed you." He then closed his eyes and fell back to sleep.

The day continued to drag on. I was exhausted from the night before. Since Jacob was asleep, I decided to nap as well. Softly, I crept to his side and made sure the covers were around him. I decided to rest on the bed close by in case he needed me. I lay down with a heavy heart. The last day and a half had been the worst I had seen so far. Soon fatigue took over, and I was asleep.

Something woke me, and I sat up with a jolt. How long had I been there? Jacob ... oh my goodness! Still a little delirious from sleep, I rushed to his side. He was still resting peacefully. His blanket had fallen from around his chest and arms and now lay on his lap. Normally, he wouldn't have let that happen and meticulously covered himself. But today was not normal. Dumbfounded, I felt his arms. They were ice cold. Fear stabbed my heart. Something was terribly wrong. I wanted to jerk him awake and make him speak to me again. I wanted to see that he was okay. But instead, I quietly pulled the covers around him and let him sleep.

Evening crept silently across the horizon, and soon darkness covered the land. The Cole house was a quiet hum of activity. Fred and Leslie were there. We had just finished discussing plans with Jacob's treatment specialist, and Fred and I went up to Jacob's room. Jacob was still completely unaware of what was going on around him. He couldn't communicate, and we couldn't wake him. When we tried to move him, he went into a seizure.

It was one of those moments that is so terrifying it almost seems surreal, but everything turns out just fine in the end. But this was very real. Jacob's face contorted, and he labored for each breath. The distance between each breath grew longer and longer until finally he didn't take another one.

In desperation, I shouted, "Breathe, Jacob! Please breathe!!!" We called 911, and I performed CPR on my husband until the paramedics arrived.

Jacob's frail body was listless, and I'm sure he felt very little of the panic in the room that night. We saw the horror of the moment, but he saw the glory, for in that room, the angel of the King stood quietly, watching, waiting, and listening for the command of His Majesty, Jesus. Life and death are in His hands. And at the ordained moment—not one too soon or too late—Jesus called Jacob's name.

The angel then took Jacob by the hand, and in an instant, they were gone. Jacob had been set free.

I, however, was not ready to let him go. I didn't understand. I believed so strongly that Jesus was going to completely heal him. How could I accept his death? I couldn't and wouldn't.

I spent the next while in fervent prayer. Jesus had raised people from the dead back in Bible times, and I knew He still could. And I expected Him to now. As I prayed, Jesus was working in my heart. Silently and without my even knowing it, Jesus was teaching me to let go. He wasn't angry about the grip I had on my husband but instead took my hand in His gentle grasp and tenderly loosened each of my fingers until I had completely let go.

Finally, I fell exhausted on the bed. I lay across Jacob's feet and buried my face into the mattress. I was silent, completely lost in thought. My mind wandered back through the past day and a half of misery. I recalled all the strange things Jacob had said during his moments of consciousness. The things he spoke didn't make much sense to me at the time but now were quite clear.

"Dawn," he said. "I dreamed I was in a race."

"Oh?" I answered. "Did you win?"

A small smile crossed his face. "Yes," he weakly nodded.

Awhile later, he said with longing, "This is so boring. Can't we speed this up?"

"Speed what up?" I asked, but he had already slipped back into his world and was too weak to answer me.

As I lay in complete silence, I suddenly knew what Jacob had been talking about. Jesus reminded him that his life on Earth was a marathon, and that he was the athlete (Hebrews 12:1–2). From the moment of receiving Christ as his Savior, Jacob had begun his marathon, ever running toward the goal that is the same for every believer in Christ. Heaven is our final objective. As a marathon is not easy and takes discipline and hard work, so is life. It requires patience and endurance as we press on. Often there are great trials and pain, but Jesus is there at the finish line, cheering us on.

Jacob was rounding the last corner of his marathon, and I pictured how Jacob saw Jesus in his dream. He was standing there with arms open wide, cheering him on. Jacob could see the angels gathered in great anticipation of his arrival and could barely wait to cross that finish line. Every fiber of his soul was stirring to go faster, but his weak body still held him captive. He longed to be free.

At that moment, my heart opened and released Jacob into the arms of God. Then and only then did I know that Jacob was gone and was not coming back. This was God's will. My man, my Prince Charming, would never be back again.

17

Hold Me, Jesus

I lost it. I fell into my mother-in-law's arms and wept. Then my own mother held me close. The whole evening is a blur to me, like a fog or a movie in slow motion. Everyone and everything became formless shadows. I screamed in agony. Finally, I lay flat in my brother's lap, sobs shaking my body. The pain was so intense I felt I would burst. I could barely breathe. "Oh my Jesus, my Jacob is gone ... is gone ... What will I do? Oh my God ... my Jesus ... help me ..."

I remember telling someone to cover Jacob's face because I couldn't bear seeing it that way anymore. Besides, I knew he wasn't there anyway. The real Jacob was far away in a place so glorious human words can't describe it.

After a long while, my sobs quieted to soft whimpers as I lay exhausted on the floor in a puddle of grief. Someone gently told me the coroner would soon arrive to take Jacob's body, and that maybe I should leave so I wouldn't have to see it. I agreed, so my mother and brother took me out for a drive. All I wanted to do was run after Jacob and be with him. I could barely stand that I was left. I had no desire to live anymore, and yet here I was.

My brother picked me up and helped walk me to the door. Before stepping out into the cold October night, I grabbed Jacob's favorite fleece jacket from the coat closet. He wore it everywhere. Pastor Dan was standing by to escort me to the waiting car. Soon I was ready, and we walked outside. When we passed my husband's truck in the driveway, a stabbing pain shot through my system. Everywhere I turned, I saw him ... thought of him ... longed for him. But he wasn't there.

Words can't describe the emptiness I felt. Even if I searched the whole world inside and out, I still wouldn't find him. When Jacob went away on a trip, I always knew where he was and that he'd be back. I was even able to call him if I needed to. However, this was completely different. I was confident of where he was (heaven), but I couldn't call him, and he wouldn't ever be coming back. Such a lonely thought.

On our drive, I looked up at the clear night sky and saw the moon shining so bright. I thought of my man and wondered what he was doing and seeing way up there in heaven's glory. Although my heart was crushed within me and the pain was intense, I was relieved that Jacob was no longer in any pain. At least I was the only one hurting now. He had suffered a great deal, but all that was in the past. I pictured his radiant face, strong and healthy. I could take the pain because I knew he was truly happy.

When I returned home, I went straight to our sons' bedroom. Caleb and Clayton were at my brother's house with Valoree while Josiah was with me. They knew nothing of the sorrow at hand. I would tell them in the morning. How I wished the morning would never come. *Couldn't we all just go see Jesus tonight?*

My mom had already put Lacey and Lydia to bed. Lacey knew nothing. For now, let her sleep. Enough sadness had already transpired for a lifetime, and I couldn't take any more. I crawled under the covers of my son's bed and lay there in the stillness. No way was I going to face my own room that night. The image of my husband's lifeless body lying on the floor with the paramedics bent over him was seared into my memory. Oh, how I wish they hadn't come. There wasn't a thing they were able to do anyway. Now, I had to try to forget it.

For the first time in months, I wasn't on duty. It was bizarre not being with him, attending to his every need. I closed my eyes and drifted in and out of sleep. I could barely wrap my mind around the events of that night and the fact that I was now a widow. How could this be? Surely this wasn't really happening but was only a horrible dream. My body lay limp and drained. The yearlong battle had taken its toll on me. I was broken inside and out, completely exhausted mentally and physically.

My dad drove over from Montana as soon as he heard the news, and he and Mom spent the night by my side. I'm their little girl, and they didn't want me to face it all alone.

The next day dawned, and my heart ached with dread. *I have to tell the children this morning.* Oh my Jesus, how could I tell the children their daddy was dead—gone and never coming back? They had prayed so diligently for him. How would they respond? Would they be angry at God? How would I be able to do this to them and crush their little hearts? Jesus would give me the words to say. His grace would cover them. And it did.

I told Lacey, our little princess, first. When she awoke, she crawled into bed with me. As she snuggled close, I stroked her hair and softly said, "Lacey, do you remember me telling you that your cousin Sabrina went to heaven a long time ago?"

She nodded her head. "Yes."

"Well," I continued. "Last night your daddy went to be with her in heaven." We continued talking as the news sunk into her little three-year-old mind. She took it well.

Soon we were joined by her brothers. When Caleb and Clayton arrived from my brother's home, they toppled into bed with me, and we all snuggled close. I told them about Daddy, and that he was now in heaven. Clayton was calm and composed. He was only four, after all. Caleb, on the other hand, began to weep. He buried his head in my chest and cried for his daddy. He was looking forward to having him back again. There were still ball games, hide-and-seek competitions, and wrestling matches to be lived out. It just couldn't be over forever. His dream was instantly shattered. His daddy was gone and wasn't coming back.

I was relieved once the children were aware of what had happened. Lacey and Clayton comforted me for a while but soon were off playing. There were so many people around to help entertain them. Eventually, even Caleb was able to dry his tears and wander off with the other children. Soon all of them were smiling again. But I was another story.

I didn't get out of bed at all that day except to make the transition from the boys' room to my own room. I needed to face it, but I didn't want anything left in there to remind me of the horrible ordeal of the night before—or the entire year, for that matter. The chair Jacob died in was promptly removed. All pills, bandages, oxygen tanks ... anything and everything having to do with his illness was taken away.

When the room was ready, I slowly walked across the hall to the closed door and placed my hand on the doorknob. I was afraid. Would it be too much for me? Could I handle being in there again? I braced myself as I pushed the door open. At that moment, God took the horror from the room and from my heart, and relief flooded over me. There was no way I would ever forget what had transpired in that room, but I wasn't haunted by it either. I placed Jacob's pictures on the table next to the bed to remind me of who he really was. I am amazed at how quickly Jesus took the horrible images of Jacob's face contorted in a seizure and replaced them with the healthy, happy ones.

My family had done a wonderful job of clearing everything away for me. I made my way to the bed and lay down on Jacob's side, the exact spot where he had spent so much time. I clung to his fleece jacket as I placed my head on his pillow.

All I can say is that Jesus held me that day. I couldn't see Him, but He was there. He saw into and felt the depths of my sorrow. The pain was still intense, and the tears came often, but Jesus never left my side.

18

Not Left Alone

It was a typical autumn day in October for Northern Idaho. The sun was not shining, or was it? I can't honestly remember, but at least it wasn't raining. The day had been hard enough without the extra jab of a rainstorm. The kids and I were in Jacob's pickup truck and were headed home from his funeral. I slowly pulled out of the church parking lot, mindful of Jacob's ski chairs in the back. They were his special hobby. He had combined two of his favorite pastimes, craftsmanship and skiing. He collected used skis, took the bindings off, and—voilà—before you knew it, what used to be something to dash down a mountain on was now a perfect spot to sit and relax. His Adirondack-style ski chairs were as sturdy as they were beautiful but not indestructible. I needed to pay attention and be sure they stayed put and didn't fall over the side of the truck as I drove.

I maneuvered into the right turn lane in preparation to enter the freeway. I was so tired. The last few days were nothing but a whirlwind of activity. I had picked myself up out of bed and poured my all into this funeral. There was the service to organize, songs to choose, photos to hunt for, a bulletin to write and deliver to the printer, questions to answer ... and this was just the tip of the iceberg.

It was almost like organizing a wedding yet completely opposite. My groom was dead and would be in a box at the altar.

Now after eight years of marriage, I stood at the back of the church once again looking at my groom—well, a picture of him sitting on top of his casket. The feelings in my heart on this day were so different from what they had been eight years ago. Then, I was bursting with joy and excitement. A wonderful life full of hopes and dreams lay in front of me. Now my heart was overflowing with sorrow and dread. My dreams had been shattered and lay in pieces all around. And yet deep inside I had an inner peace. From my perspective, my life was spinning out of control—my control. But not out of God's. He was still in perfect control of everything.

I picked up speed as I drove down the on-ramp. The day had been a blur. The service and reception turned out beautifully—if you can use that word to describe a funeral. I planned it the way I knew Jacob would want it. He loved Jesus with all his heart and would want nothing more than for his funeral to reflect that. People came from near and far to honor his memory. In fact, several times I thought what a bummer it was that Jacob couldn't have been there too. Being the people person he was, he would have enjoyed seeing everyone.

It's a strange feeling being at your husband's funeral. I felt awkward and alone. There were people everywhere, offering hugs and sweet words, and yet, I felt so alone. Jacob wasn't at my side to share in the conversations. He wasn't sitting at the table when I returned with a plate of food during the reception. He wasn't there to lean on when I felt my body grow weary. He was not there, period. I wanted so desperately to crawl into a hole and hide. I was drained physically and emotionally.

I eased the truck onto the freeway. I knew I needed to maintain my speed so as not to annoy the other drivers, but my cargo in the back was very precious. I couldn't go too fast or something might happen. Jacob's ski chairs had been on display in the foyer of the church. I thought it fitting to bring in a few items to remind people of who he was. I also added his personal skis, boots, and accessories to the display. It looked lovely and shouted his name from ski tip to boot buckle.

This whole "driving these chairs down the middle of the freeway" thing was not my cup of tea. It stressed me out. Jacob would be doing this if he were here. He was always the one to cover for me and do the more difficult things. Either one of Jacob's brothers would have covered for me in a second, but I needed to do this.

I still could hardly believe this was happening. A young, thirty-one-year-old woman with four small children is not supposed to be driving home from her husband's funeral. She is supposed to be cooking dinner for him when he returns from work each night, planning a picnic lunch to spend with him at the park during his lunch break, or taking pictures of him and the kids hard at work in the sandbox. I was supposed to be going on dates with the man I loved, laughing at his silly jokes, and planning what we wanted to do for our tenth anniversary. This reality was not the way it was supposed to be, but it was. This was my new normal.

Suddenly, I heard a crash, and my heart skipped a beat. The chairs! What had happened? I looked in the rearview mirror. Oh, good. They were both still there! However, something must have shifted. I didn't know what had happened. Were the chairs on the brink of falling over? Fortunately, I was near an off-ramp, so I exited the freeway and slowly pulled into the nearest gas station.

I opened the door to get out, hoping I would be strong enough to lug the chairs back into the right position. It was then that it hit me with full force. "Dawn, you are alone. Jacob is gone." Even though I had been walking as a widow for six whole days now, it was the first time I was truly *alone*. The reality swept over me with a wave of sorrow as I thought, *This is how it will be from now on. Jacob is not here to help me anymore. He is not here to rescue me from my predicaments. I have to figure stuff out now. Yup, even the "man" stuff—like here and now.*

As I climbed into the back of the truck to adjust the chairs, I didn't see Jesus climb up there with me. I didn't see Him put His hand over mine, giving me the strength to pull those heavy chairs. I didn't see Him push them into a steady position for me. And I didn't see Him sitting there the whole way home, protecting them for me. But most definitely, He was there. If I had been given the eyes to see, I would have seen Jesus that day. And if I had been able to peer into the future, I would have seen Him there as well. His amazing grace was upon me, holding me. I would never be truly alone.

19

The Aftermath

After the funeral, the children and I went to Montana to stay with my parents. I was completely exhausted physically and emotionally and needed my family. I wasn't ready to be a full-time single mom just yet. I needed time to rest, grieve, and begin to heal. The situation was perfect. I could be there for my kids in their grief and also have help in caring for them.

All color had been stripped from my life. I lived in a gray scale world now. Nothing really mattered anymore except the important things like Jesus and those I loved. The petty things that once seemed so important or desirable meant nothing to me anymore. The pain was excruciating. It completely encompassed my whole being. At times, all I could do was curl up in a ball under the blankets and weep. Salty tears would flow in rivers down my cheeks and onto my lips as sobs shook my body. Eventually, fatigue would take over and I would grow quiet, but I still always felt hollow inside. The hole in my heart was a vast crater.

In my tremendous grief, though, I knew I wasn't alone. God's Word promises that Jesus will always be with us (Matthew 28:20). He poured His grace upon me and filled me with new strength. After my breakdowns, He helped me get up and live another hour and then another. The pain was still there, but somehow I was able to continue on with the next thing at hand, whether it was dressing a child, taking a shower, or making breakfast. God's grace always brought me through.

There came a point when I knew it was time to return to our home in Idaho. Our family needed regrouping, and it had been a long time since we were a normal family doing normal things. The kids needed me to gather them together and lead them forward. How in the world was I supposed to do that alone? At times, anger rose up with in my heart. "Jacob, how dare you leave me alone to pick up all these pieces and try to put our home back in order!" I even went so far as to dare to think, *Here you are now without a care in the world, and I am left to toil and struggle on. It's not fair!*

These thoughts were always brief and were gone almost as soon as they arose, but nonetheless, they still came. How silly, right? As if Jacob had a choice in the matter. He would never have chosen to leave me alone to wade through this mire of grief. I wasn't really angry at him; it was just an expression of the pain I felt inside.

Anger is a very normal part of grief. Some experience it more than others since every loss is different. We are simply human and think as humans do. However, what we decide to do with our anger is crucial to the healing process. We can either hold onto it because we feel we have the right to be angry or we can let go and hand it over to God.

A serious physical wound that hasn't been properly cleaned may become infected. If vital measures aren't quickly taken to treat the infection, it will only grow worse and become potentially life threatening. It's the same with anger. If we hold onto it, we will miss the beauty Jesus wants to bring out of our grief. We will not heal but will only fester in our pain, and if we continue to forbid Jesus to clean our wound, our lives will grow seriously worse as bitterness sets in. However, if we give our anger to Jesus, we will experience inner healing and peace. In doing this, we release the plan we had for our lives—what we wanted—and instead say, "Jesus, I trust You no matter what. I don't understand why You have allowed it to go this way, but I trust You have a reason I can't see." But *we* have to make this decision to let go, for God will not force us to surrender. Rest assured, though, He does walk us through the letting go.

But even this doesn't mean we will instantly accept our situation or that the pain will simply vanish. It won't. But we will begin to heal and feel peace inside knowing that Jesus holds our world in His hands. We may not agree with His choice in the matter, but we can rest assured that His Word promises "...all things work together for good to them that love God, to them who are the called according to his purpose" (Romans 8:28). Little by little, joy will return, and we will glorify Jesus as we see the work He has done in our lives. Beauty will come from ashes (Isaiah 61:3).

The Lord put determination within my heart to keep being the parent He wanted me to be. Whether Jacob was there or not, I had a job to do. I had a calling on my life, and I couldn't bail out now. I wanted to honor my husband and continue to lead our children in this life.

More times than not, though, all I wanted was to die and go be with my husband. I never once seriously contemplated suicide. I only wished that something would just happen *to* me. But in my heart, I knew Jacob wouldn't want that. As much as we loved each other, he would want me to be here with our children. They needed me. Besides, there was no way I would truly wish the loss of two parents on my beautiful babies. They had been through enough.

I still held purpose in this life even though my husband had fulfilled his. He lived out all God had planned for him to do and accomplish on this earth, and through it, he brought God glory. It was now his time to go home. It wasn't my time yet. As much as I yearned to be with Jacob, I yearned even more to fulfill my calling, my purpose. I wanted to "finish my race with joy" like the apostle Paul wanted to do when he penned these words so many hundreds of years ago, "But none of these things move me, neither count I my life dear unto myself, so that I might finish my course with joy, and the ministry, which I have received of the Lord Jesus, to testify the gospel of the grace of God" (Acts 20:24).

It pained me to think of fulfilling this calling without Jacob here with me. He and I were so much a part of one another. There was a great deal we wanted to do together for Jesus on this earth and in this life.

Then I realized that Jacob was still in me and in our children. His legacy would live on through all of us. Picking up the Cole family baton and keep running for Jacob and for Jesus was an honor. Jacob's purpose in life still lived on in me. "All for His glory, Dawn. Keep running for the glory of Jesus."

20

Homecoming

I began making preparations to return home, but before I could face walking into that house again, there were a few things that needed to be done. The most important one was that I wanted the furniture in my bedroom rearranged. I'd never be able to forget all that took place in that room—all the sorrow and pain—but it would help ease the memories if it looked different. *Really* different.

I called a friend who had graciously offered to help in any way she could. I filled her in on my plan to return home and then shared my desires with her. She agreed to help and soon set to work to meet my requests. What a blessing to have someone to call upon in time of need! Through the whole ordeal of Jacob's illness, God made sure we had plenty of supportive friends. Loving people had given of themselves on our behalf. Meals came night after night for months. Our house was cleaned, the children were cared for, and even the vast amount of produce used in Jacob's diet was lovingly washed week after week.

Now the battle was over, and I didn't need the same kind of help anymore. Oh, I still had needs alright, but they were different now. I could cook and clean on my own once again, but I knew that when-ever an issue arose, I had amazing friends and family who would be there for me. Their love and support was still very much alive. I will always be grateful for their faithfulness during the hardest time of our lives.

My heart was now at peace knowing that things in Idaho were being taken care of in preparation for our homecoming. Next, it was time to get organized on the Montana side. I began packing the kids' clothing and toys. How often I had done this in the past, as our family frequented Grandpa and Grandma's house on many occasions. At times, Jacob's commitments kept him home and I made the journey alone with the children. We always had a lovely time, but it was always just as lovely to pack up and return home to a waiting husband and father who scooped us up in his arms, excited to see us again.

But this time, I prepared myself for a very different homecoming. Jacob wouldn't be standing in the doorway with a big smile and a huge embrace that said, "Welcome home, I missed you guys." There wouldn't be any of that ... because Jacob was gone forever. Our home was merely an empty shell that now only echoed what once was and what would never be again.

The day of our departure arrived. I had planned to return to Montana eventually, but for now this trip was necessary. It wasn't easy leaving my comfort zone and taking steps of my own again. The full weight of it all was on my shoulders, but I was confident that Jesus would provide the grace I needed to face each moment in the coming days. And so, after warm good-byes and many hugs, Caleb, Clayton, Lacey, Lydia, and I set off on our journey.

Darkness had fallen by the time we arrived. The air was chilly, although no snow had fallen yet this December. We stopped by Fred and Leslie's house first and were lovingly welcomed home. The kids ran around and played after being cooped up in the car for so long. They were eager to be back once again and see their papa and nana.

After some time, we said our good nights and headed to our house. As we neared our home, the kids grew antsy in their seats and cried excitedly. "Christmas lights! Oh, Mommy, look! Christmas lights!"

Our house stood draped with icicle lights from eave to eave. It looked beautiful as it twinkled in the darkness and was far from what I'd expected to see as I rounded the bend. It didn't look cold and forsaken after all but rather warm and cheerful, as if we'd never been away. Maybe this homecoming wouldn't be so hard after all.

I opened the garage door, pulled the van in, and parked. The kids tumbled out, bounced through the door, and into the house. Bracing myself, I followed them in. When I opened the door and took my first step inside, I felt a surge of joy and peace. My eyes widened in wonder and utter amazement as I looked around. I only asked for a few simple favors but much more than that had been done.

The lights were on, and the house was warm. A large Christmas tree stood glowing in the corner. Nearly every room in the house held a surprise of some kind, as if our home had undergone a makeover. The children giggled and shrieked in delight as they ran from room to room. Rooms were painted and curtains hung. There were cute lamps and decorations all over. The house looked incredible and totally made up for the things Jacob and I hadn't the time to finish.

By this time, I was more than eager to see what had been done with my room. When I entered and looked around, my heart melted. I felt joy instead of the searing pain I was expecting. There wasn't a flood of sorrowful memories to torment my soul but instead a warm embrace of love wrapped itself around me. My room had been transformed from hospital gray into elegant beauty. The furniture had been rearranged, the walls painted, and curtains hung. My bed was spiced up with a new comforter and pillow set. It was lovely beyond words.

My heart sang. The dreaded homecoming was filled with the grace of Jesus. His love had been poured upon us through many loving volunteers and generous donations that made this all possible. Words couldn't express the thankfulness I felt inside. As I crawled into my cozy new pj's and slippers, I knew I was loved.

21

Dealing with Sorrow

The sun came up on time the next morning and the next, whether I was glad to see it or not. Life at the Cole house continued, and although I didn't feel much like being a mom, it was essential. My kids needed me to draw us together and figure out how to be a family again. There were discipline issues to be dealt with and attitudes that needed adjusting. I'd been so busy over the last year trying to juggle everything at once that many things fell between the cracks. The task at hand would require my full attention.

I also realized how vital it was for my children to have some "Mom Time." Although I tried to seize every opportunity to spend with them during Jacob's illness, I knew it hadn't been sufficient. Now there was plenty of time to spend reading, playing games, or telling stories. I politely made it known that I wouldn't be taking visitors for the present since I needed time alone with my kids.

Mostly, I lacked my previous joy and zest for motherhood. I wasn't a very fun mom at present; however, I was a determined one. I could do this. I *must* do it! Not in my own strength but in God's. I desperately needed Him moment by moment. There were days when I felt as if a thousand pounds lay at the bottom of my heart, weighing it down. My whole world had completely changed. My bubble of hope for Jacob's full recovery had popped when he died. Dreams I had for our family lay shattered at my feet. What in the world would become of us now? But however grim things looked to me, I wouldn't let go of the hope I had in God.

I believed with all my heart that what had befallen our family wasn't by mistake. Jesus hadn't let the ball drop with an "Ooops! Sorry about that! I didn't see that one coming!" It wasn't an accident, nor was it a lack of God's power. God holds all things in His hands, and nothing can touch one of His children without His permission.

I'm not saying God sent cancer into my husband's body to kill him. But I am saying He allowed it. He could've stopped it at any moment, and I don't understand why He didn't. Jacob and I believed with all our hearts that nothing is impossible for God. We prayed and pleaded again and again as well as did countless others. Our faith hadn't ever been stronger, nor had we believed more dedicatedly than we did then. And yet God withheld His healing hand. Why?

Well, we can search the world inside and out and completely exhaust ourselves trying to find the answer. Or we can keep it really simple. God is God and does what He wants. We can't comprehend His ways and wisdom. They are beyond our understanding. Isaiah 55:8–9 says it well, "'For my thoughts are not your thoughts, neither are your ways my ways,' saith the LORD. 'FOR AS THE HEAVENS ARE HIGHER THAN THE EARTH, SO ARE MY WAYS HIGHER THAN YOUR WAYS, and my thoughts than your thoughts.'"

For many of us, this isn't an answer we readily embrace. Instead, we hold it at arm's length, seeking a better one. We want a more tangible answer, one we can wrap our "own understanding" around and see with our eyes. We continue searching and yet never find. We continue to be in turmoil and unrest, not wanting to yield. For many of us, it may take years or even a lifetime, before our hearts finally say, "Jesus I will trust You even though I can't see why You allowed it." God's Word so wisely says, "Trust in the LORD with all thine heart; and lean not unto thine own understanding. In all thy ways acknowledge Him, and He shall direct thy paths" (Proverbs 3:5–6).

God's Word cautions us not to depend on our own understanding but to simply trust Him and acknowledge His sovereignty in the matter. In times of weakness, we may still question, "But why?????" And there will still be tears, sorrow, and pain. However, in those times of weakness, we have this promise to cling to: "And we know that all things work together for good to them that love God, to them who are the called according to His purpose" (Romans 8:28). We can be confident knowing that Jesus will never allow anything into our life without a purpose. He is always working for our good.

However, we must let go of any preconceptions of what "for good" in our lives will look like. If we don't, we will become disappointed and discouraged and eventually be tempted to stop believing. We must be patient.

Jesus isn't finished with our family but will somehow use this heartbreak for our good, as crazy as that sounds. But it's what the Bible says, and I'll take God's word for it. He will use this to make us stronger in Him, and through it, He will be glorified. More than anything, I want Jesus to be seen in us; for Him to be seen as strong in our weakness, joy in our sorrow, and life in the midst of death. He can take tragedy and turn it into triumph because He has a bigger plan than we can possibly imagine.

Life without pain sounds glorious, but unfortunately it's not possible. Not yet anyway. One day in heaven it will be, but in the here and now, Jesus uses misfortune to build strength within our hearts and lives. He molds us into individuals of integrity who have chosen to trust Him even when everything around us appears hopeless. If everything were always perfect without trials, what kind of people would we be? I think you know the answer to that one.

Adversity isn't pleasant, but it can produce great beauty in a life that allows it to. A diamond is a stone of exquisite splendor. After it has been cut and polished, it sparkles and shimmers. However, this magnificent gem was first formed deep in the earth under great pressure and intense heat. It's the same with people. Trials of tremendous pressure and heat can be used to form lives into something of brilliant beauty that radiates the faithfulness of God.

Be patient, anchor into His Word, and you will not be defeated.

Jesus will send encouragement and strength along the way as He faithfully continues to work in your life for your good. It will hold a glorious, eternal value, and its worth will far exceed the world's wealth in riches and pleasures. Your faith will be strong and pure, and in it, Jesus will be glorified. First Peter 1:6–7 says,

"Wherein ye greatly rejoice, though now for a season, if need be ye are in heaviness through manifold temptations: That the trial of your faith, being much more precious than of gold that perisheth, though it be tried by fire, might be found unto praise and honour and glory at the appearing of Jesus Christ."

This concept is more challenging to explain to children, but I did my best and hoped God would make it clear to them. We also talked of heaven and the happy days ahead we have to look forward to. One day, we would see Daddy again. This helped bring joy and hope into our gloomy moments, and although the children couldn't spend their lifetime on Earth with their dad, they would one day spend eternity with him. Eternity is a long time—plenty of time to make up for the lost moments here on Earth.

The more we talked of heaven, the more we wanted to know. Heaven became so real to our family. It had always been a place of wonder but wasn't something we talked about much. Now it was the daily subject of an amazing world where not only Jesus was waiting for us, but also my beloved husband and their beloved dad. Death wasn't a feared subject for my children as it shouldn't be for any of God's people. It is simply a switch from one reality into the next; from a place of sojourning to one permanent and eternal. It's the leaving behind of a mediocre existence for one that is brilliant, perfect, and amazing in every way.

Heaven is definitely something God's people should be excited about. He's been preparing it for a long time (John 14:2–3). If God made such a beautiful earth in only seven days, just think what heaven will be like after all this time. I think we as Christians often have a misconception about heaven. In our limited thinking, we tend to picture ourselves floating on clouds and feeling … well, kind of bored. But the Bible has much more to say about heaven than we realize if we just take the time to search it out. We'll be anything but bored as we walk those streets of gold and gasp in sheer wonder at all Jesus has prepared for us. It'll be an amazing adventure where we'll live on in peace and harmony forever as we worship Jesus our Savior.

Knowing that God had a purpose in what had befallen us and that one day we'd be with Jacob again helped the children and me deal with our sorrow. It brought strength to remain in the here and now. But it sure was lonely without him around. To help ease this pain, I often played home videos from the days when Daddy was still with us. The kids gobbled them up and begged for more. Seeing Jacob in action once again was a delight. He'd been sick for almost a year, and for children, that's a long time. Their memories of him happy and strong were fading quickly, so home videos brought them back to life in their minds' eye. I am so thankful for all the effort I put into taking videos during our happy years as a family.

Seeing their father and my husband on the TV screen brought joy to our melancholy days. Hearing his voice again throughout the house was such a delight. I wanted to grab the kids and run through the screen and back in time. However, if we live in the past, we will not grow into the future God has planned for us but will be stuck going around and around. I couldn't return to the days gone by, but I knew in time I would learn to be thankful for what used to be and look forward to what was still to come.

22

I'll Never Quit

The children seemed to be adjusting well to our new life—life without dad. Of course they continued to miss him and have moments of tears, but I was relieved to see they didn't seem to be harboring bitterness. I continued praying for them that Jesus would minister to their hearts in such a way that they'd never become resentful of Him. The last thing I wanted was for our children to think, "God didn't answer our prayer. He didn't make Dad better. I have no use for Him now."

To this day, I've never heard those words come out of my children's mouths. I thank God for this and will continue to pray that as they grow and reflect on their father's death their hearts will remain open to His sovereignty and will see how Jesus uses trials in our lives for our good and for His glory. If they do begin to question, I trust that Jesus will be right by their side, holding their hands, and guiding them into complete healing and peace.

However, behavioral issues were another matter. Their attitudes and manners desperately needed my attention. At times, I became frustrated that Jacob wasn't here to help when I needed him most. Good parenting is no easy task even on the best of days, let alone now while trying to adjust to doing it alone. I no longer had anyone to bounce issues off of or to go to for advice. There wasn't a partnership anymore. I was the Lone Ranger now and hated it with a passion.

But quitting wasn't an option. A job needed to be done, and I was going to do it. I was possessive of this task and wasn't very open to outside help or advice. I wasn't against help from Jesus—there was no way I could do it without Him. However, it irritated me when others offered counsel. I eventually outgrew this stage, but at the beginning, that's where I stood. It angered me because it was Jacob's job to help me, not anyone else. He'd always been the head of this home, and these were his children. He was supposed to be here. Slowly over time, I learned to release him and let him go. His heart for his kids would live on inside me, and I would raise them the way he would have wished. But he would never be back to help me.

At times, my new reality combined with the ever-present craving to be held in Jacob's arms, hear his voice, and look into his eyes was almost too much to bear. My heart screamed in agony. My soul mate was gone. How could I possibly take another breath without him? Occasionally, I went into our closet and grabbed an armload of his shirts that hung there, unused. I stood holding them and buried my face deep into the cloth, desperately trying to be close to him, to smell his scent. I sobbed and screamed in bitter anguish as I clung to all that was left of him.

Everywhere I went and in everything I did, Jacob was in my heart. Driving around town was a constant reminder of him. Memories flashed through my mind as I recognized places we'd been. Around this corner was the park where we played when Caleb was a toddler. Along this freeway lay the bike path where the boys rode their bikes as Jacob and I pushed Lacey in the stroller. And that restaurant was where we purchased shakes one hot summer day and drove around town because our car was air-conditioned and our home wasn't.

It took awhile before I could face driving to Riverstone, Jacob's former place of employment. Riverstone built high end condos and had several nearly finished and many more to come. Jacob was the supervisor who completed the checklist on each condominium, making sure everything was in order from ceiling to floor and that the owners were satisfied. Employers and condo owners alike respected Jacob. His employer knew he could be trusted to do what was asked of him and then some. Condo owners appreciated that he always made their needs a priority. In fact, Jacob had hung a sign above his desk in his office that said, "Others." This was his reminder to treat others with respect and dignity and to serve them the best he could.

The children and I often stopped by to say hi or to eat lunch together. Jacob's face lit up every time we came. He loved showing us his latest project or condo inspection. Every now and then, I took the children to the park across from Riverstone where sometimes he joined us for a picnic lunch and a quick kiss and hug.

So it goes without explaining how difficult it was for me to face this area again. I couldn't bear driving over there knowing that Jacob wouldn't be around the next corner to greet me. His office was dark and silent, and his parking spot was empty. However, one evening I happened to be in the area when a sudden surge of courage shot through me, and I decided to face my fear. I needed to take this step in the healing process. Sometimes, when we hurt so deeply, it's easier to avoid what brings us pain, but often it's just what we need to face in order for healing to come.

It was early evening, and darkness had fallen. I gripped the steering wheel, turned my car toward Riverstone, and made my way down the long road that led into the parking lot. As I pulled in and slowly drove around the development, tears welled up, spilled over, and ran in torrents down my cheeks. I gazed around, drinking in each memory as it came to me. Slowly, the stabbing pain turned to a dull ache. As I pressed into the pain, it began to subside. I would need several more trips to Riverstone and months of healing before the pain was replaced with simply joyful memories, but the process began that night. God's presence was with me, holding me close.

No matter how difficult it was to rear the children on my own or how painful it was to face the memories of the past, I never quit. Jesus was holding me each step of the way, and little by little, I was growing stronger and stronger.

23

Adjustments

By mid-December, I felt the kids and I had bonded well enough to incorporate social events once again. It was time to take another step forward and reach out to those who loved us so much. They had respectfully given us the space we needed, and now it was time to show them we were okay and were going to make it.

At first, it was a challenge being around our circle of friends. Most were married and had families. I was suddenly the odd duck and felt out of place. It was weird being among them and feeling that alone. I had never felt that way before. They never did or said anything that made me feel the slightest bit left out or unloved; they were caring and kind as always. The problem wasn't with them but with me. I had changed, and it wasn't anyone's fault. It was simply just the way it was.

One night, it really hit me as I prepared for our pastor, his wife, and kids to arrive for dinner. It was the first time I had the energy to entertain someone besides family, but I was only serving take-and-bake pizza and salad. At one time, I had been quite a cook and enjoyed preparing delicious things for my family. But now without Jacob, what was the point? He was the one I made things special for anyway. Now that it was just the children and me, I didn't have that same desire. My grocery list included as many premade and frozen dinners as possible, and it was okay. This was where I was in life. I needed things kept simple. I even bought frozen cookie dough, which I'd *never* done before. If Jacob knew I wasn't making chocolate chip cookies from scratch, he would've been shocked!

The doorbell rang. Our guests were here. We greeted each other with hugs and cheerful hellos. It was great seeing them all again. They removed their coats and made their way into the living room. Their three children ran off to play with my older three. Baby Lydia was too young yet to join the group, so she stayed with the adults.

Now if Jacob had been there, he and Dan would have made themselves at home in the living room and soon found several notable topics to discuss, several of them humorous. Sounds of their cheerful voices and laughter would have drifted into the kitchen where Nicole and I would be chatting and preparing to serve the meal. But tonight wasn't that way because Jacob was gone.

Dan was very understanding. He joined Nicole and I in conversation and helped out with the kids. It was just like old times ... except it wasn't. There was definitely a huge void without Jacob there, and his absence was noticeable. No one said anything, but everyone felt it.

As the pizza baked, I opened the cupboard doors and began removing the plates and glasses we'd need. Without thinking, I grabbed six small plates and glasses for the children and then reached for larger ones for the adults. All of a sudden, I realized I had placed four large plates and glasses on the counter. It had always been that way—two for Jacob and me and two for our guests. I had done it out of habit. Embarrassed, I quickly put the extra setting away, hoping I hadn't been seen. Yes, this whole "being alone" thing would take some getting used to.

The evening progressed and eventually ended well. Everyone left with smiles on their faces. I had just entertained my first dinner guests as a widow. Jesus had pulled me through, but I looked with distaste upon my new title. I could barely say the words, "I am a widow."

Caleb told me one day, "Mom, the word *widow* doesn't fit you."

"It doesn't sound right, does it?" I replied.

A widow is supposed to be a darling grandma with silvery hair who had lived a full life with the man of her dreams before he slipped away and was gone. But I wasn't old. I was still young. Jacob and I hadn't lived out what we thought to be a full lifetime. It had been too short. I wasn't ready to be a widow yet and left standing alone during this season in life when I desperately needed my husband.

The emotions I experienced during those first months of being single were astounding. For some reason, I suddenly felt shy and embarrassed. In public, I wanted to slink away and hide. Often when I was greeted, people were first drawn to my children, which is natural, of course. I was thankful to hide behind their cuteness and avoid a lot of those "How are you?" questions people liked to ask.

Jacob and I were soul mates; truly two people entwined as one. Without him, I felt only half there. For years, Jacob and I had been leaning on one another and working as a team. Suddenly, my support was taken away. I was still teetering back and forth, trying to compensate as I learned how to stand on my own. I had depended so much on him. Fortunately, I'm a very determined person, and with Jesus as my source of strength, I would find a way to keep this family going. We would continue to meet challenges and go through adjustments, but everything would work out in the end because with Jesus Christ all things are possible.

24

Time Alone (2010)

Once Christmas and New Years were over, I reevaluated how things were going in our family and what the next step should be. The children were doing much better. There will never come a day in parenting when we can just hang up our apron and say, "Well now, my kids are perfect and will stay that way from here on out." That would be nice, but it won't ever happen.

Each of my children still had individual issues that I continued working on, but overall, I had accomplished a great deal by slowing down and spending time with them. They felt secure knowing that although dad was gone, mom was still here. But I wasn't the same mom they had known in the past. I lacked the sparkle and vigor I once possessed. I suppose it was still in me somewhere, but it needed time to be revived. A long time …

I often apologized to my kids for being short and irritable with them. "Mommy is having a hard time right now," I tried to explain. "I miss Daddy so much." They seemed to understand. After all, they were pretty used to seeing me that way.

Grief came in waves. Some days were definitely lighter and easier to face. But there were also moments when sorrow came crashing down upon me with the force of an enormous tidal wave. I struggled, gasping for air, as the riptide pulled me under and deeper and deeper into the depths of grief. During these moments, I cried out, "Jesus, help me! Jesus, help me!" This was all I had the strength to say. Life looked as vast as the Grand Canyon stretching out before me, and I was overwhelmed by it all. As I looked at my boys bounding with energy, Lacey trying to keep up with them, and baby Lydia needing so much care, I thought, *How can I do it?*

There was laundry to be done, dishes to wash, diapers to change, hungry mouths to feed, sticky fingers to clean, and that was just the beginning. Often, I only had enough strength to crawl through the day. Of course, I don't literally mean on my hands and knees. I lacked the energy it took to stand and walk. If all I could do was crawl through each difficult hour then that was what I would do. I confidently held the hand of Jesus, knowing He would never let me go. Every time I called His name, He was right there. I'm not saying the storm instantly vanished and the sun came out. Far from it. Usually, everything stayed the same or grew worse. However, in those moments, God always gave me the perfect measure of grace I needed to make it through the rest of the day.

Upon evaluation, I concluded that the kids were doing well. *I* was the one who was struggling. I desperately wanted to be alone, just Jesus and me. I needed to grieve whenever and however it came about. My heart, mind, and body pleaded for a complete rest and the opportunity to relax—a chance to be alone to think and pray for direction for our future.

With all this in mind, I began to pack for Montana. I asked my parents to watch the children while I went to a nearby cabin resort. This would be my first time away completely by myself. It may sound lonely or weird to some, but I was looking forward to it with great anticipation.

The children and I said our good-byes to our Idaho family and made the trip back to the land of the cowboy. I stayed around long enough to make sure the kids were settled with my parents. After everyone was A-OK, I packed my bags and hopped into the car.

It was early evening when I pulled out of the driveway. The rays of the setting sun fell across the snowy mountains, changing them from a dazzling white into a soft rose and then back to white again as the sky began to darken. How beautiful it was.

I pulled the car into the parking spot near my cabin just as darkness fell. I unloaded my bags and stepped onto the front porch, not knowing what to expect when I placed my key in the lock and pushed the door open. What would vacation be like alone? I'd been looking forward to it for so long, but now that it was here, I wasn't sure.

I stepped inside and closed the door behind me. I gazed around and felt a warm glow rising in my heart. The lights were on, and the flames of the gas fireplace flickered cheerfully. The warmth of the room enveloped me, and immediately, I thought of Jacob and wished he could be there with me. But I would be okay because Jesus had walked into that room with me. He would be there to hold, encourage, and comfort me. His strength would fill my body, enabling me to keep walking through whatever the future held for the children and me. He would give me wisdom for the decisions that lay ahead.

25

Good-bye

Within a few days, my respite came to an end. It had been a beautiful retreat, but it was time to face reality once again. Jesus and I had connected in a special way. He gave me courage for the next step in life, my body and mind had been able to rest, and yes, I shed tears by the bucketful. But I emerged victorious in the end.

For a while I had been trying to decide whether I should move to Montana permanently or remain in Idaho. What was best for the children? For me? I wanted to sell our house. It held very few fond memories since we hadn't lived in it long enough to make many. But after it sold, what were we to do?

During my time at the cabin, I made several decisions for our immediate future. I would put our home in Idaho up for sale and return to Montana to find a place to rent. Living close to my parents seemed like a great idea. However, so much of what we knew and loved was still in Idaho. Our time in the rental would provide a chance to decide exactly what we should do. If I felt it best to return to Idaho, we could simply pick up and go. However, if we were supposed to stay, I could easily go in that direction with a more permanent dwelling. I felt confident about this decision and proceeded in that direction.

The children and I soon returned to Idaho to prepare our home to place on the market. It already looked beautiful thanks to its transformation back in December, but it still needed several finishing touches. I added a picture here or a candle there to areas that needed a bit more sparkle. I wanted my home to be as appealing as possible in hopes of attracting a buyer.

Then there was the family room issue that needed to be addressed. Jacob hadn't the chance to complete the trim work around the two entry doors, and it didn't look finished the way it was. I wasn't about to tackle that, so I called on a special friend. My husband and Jake had been friends for years, and I knew he could be trusted. Within a couple days, Jake had the trim on, and it looked amazing!

Next, I sorted through and cleaned closets, drawers, and cupboards. Then when the house sold, everything would be easier to pack. It was a lot of hard work and effort, but it's what I needed at the time. I wanted to stay busy. An idle mind can be such a hindrance to healthy healing.

Finally, with every last detail finished, I placed the sale of our home into the hands of Caroline, who not only was a family friend, but my trusted realtor as well. With great satisfaction, I closed the door, and once again, the kids and I were off to Montana.

It didn't take long to find a rental. I settled on a large furnished home with a huge backyard that spread out over a couple acres and finally ended at the edge of a small lake. Towering behind it was the Swan Mountain Range. What an amazing view! The neighborhood was quiet with each home spread out for an adequate amount of privacy. It was peaceful … just what I needed.

February soon rolled into March as the kids and I made ourselves at home in our new temporary house. There was plenty of room for the kids to roam around as the weather outside did its best to warm into spring. Eventually, the trees began to bud, the grass greened up, and the sweet scent of flowers filled the air. I often wonder what it's like for Jacob in heaven. I'm sure the flowers there are incredible. The grass, mountains, brooks—everything must be gorgeous and full of the vibrancy of eternal life.

As our weather warmed up, I loved sitting on the back deck and gazing into the sky. I'd dream of my man and wonder, "What are you doing right now?" I often thought, *Wow! I mean, wow! Jacob, you know what Jesus looks like! You have touched His hands and looked Him right in the eyes. He has spoken to you face to face!* The magnitude of it all sometimes overwhelmed me. My husband had been given the honor of all honors—free access into the throne room of His Majesty, Jesus Christ.

Spring gave way to summer and with it came the happy news of an offer on our home in Idaho. It was more of a buyer's market than a seller's, but I was able to get enough out of the house to make it worth my while. I was overjoyed the Lord had allowed it to sell so quickly.

Signing the final papers without Jacob was difficult. In fact, the whole ordeal of selling this house had been a growing experience for me. But my realtor was such a blessing throughout the entire process. Caroline was there for me every step of the way. Having someone you trust is vital when treading down such an unfamiliar path.

I needed a couple weeks to pack things up. I didn't want to be rushed. After all, this was a huge deal, a tremendous undertaking without my husband there to help. I spent a good while simply gathering boxes and organizing anything I hadn't already done during my visit in the spring. Next, I called on friends and family who had offered to help. Jacob may not have been able to be there, but I definitely wasn't alone.

I rented a storage locker and put all our belonging in there temporarily. Since the home I was renting in Montana was fully furnished, we didn't need our belongings. If I decided to buy a house again, I would come for our things at that point.

I wanted to be the one who packed Jacob's things, so while others packed our stuff in boxes, I concentrated on packing his. I'd given some of his clothing and shoes to his father, brothers, and close friends and saved a bunch for the children. A friend of mine offered to make memory quilts out of Jacob's dress shirts for each of our four children. Anything remaining after that I stored in boxes for later. I couldn't possibly take them to the thrift store or throw them away.

Sorting through the garage was my last undertaking. It was filled with Jacob's tools, skis, hobby items, and camping supplies. I smiled as memories flooded over me. He was so much a part of the items in this room. I could hear his voice as he chatted with a neighbor who had stopped by to check out his latest project. I could see him hovered over his drill press as he constructed his ski chairs. I could feel the warmth of his love as he skillfully labored over a project he was working on for me. It was a walk down memory lane for sure as I sorted and packed that day. I saved almost everything that was Jacob's.

Before I knew it, everything in our home had been packed and moved out. The empty rooms echoed from the children's voices as they ran around delighted for so much free space to roam. This would be our last night in this house, for tomorrow I would hand in our keys, and the home would no longer belong to us. Fred and Leslie invited us to sleep at their house that night knowing all the beds were gone from ours. However, I needed to spend our last night together there in that house. I was just fine with the floor, a few blankets, and a pillow. We needed this time to say good-bye.

The kids and I all snuggled together on the floor in Caleb and Clayton's room. We talked about our life and this house. We remembered the times we visited it as it was being constructed. Then the subject switched to Dad. We missed him so very much. I shared in more detail about the night he died. Since it happened suddenly and at night, the kids weren't around. All they knew was that Dad was here one day and gone the next. They hadn't even been able to say good-bye. I wanted to give them a child-sized version of what took place that night.

I was quite sure that saying good-bye to this house wouldn't be a big deal for me. After all, so many of the memories made there I wanted to forget anyway. We had moved in with so many hopeful dreams—dreams that hadn't come to pass and never would. Therefore, it surprised me when I began to feel that dreadful lump of sorrow rise up in my throat. How could this be? I didn't doubt my decision to sell (and still don't to this day), and yet I was having a hard time letting go. True, our brief time there had been one of trial, but I still felt a stabbing pain knowing that it was another part of Jacob that would be gone forever. Soon the children's eyes closed for the night, and I was left to walk the rest of memory lane alone until eventually I, too, fell asleep.

The next day was filled with scurrying here and cleaning there. Friends and family had come to help, making sure I didn't have to do everything alone. By evening, the house looked amazing and was spotless. I even left some flowers on the counter to welcome the new homeowners. I wanted them to walk in and instantly feel right at home. In the short conversations I had had with them, I could tell they were in love with the house and would take good care of it. Our home was being left in good hands. Jacob would be supporting this decision of mine in every way. I felt such relief knowing that in a matter of moments all this would be over, and I would walk out that door for the last time. I had done it ... with the help of Jesus and many wonderful people.

I took one last look around. Gulping down my sorrow, I placed the keys on the counter, turned toward the door, opened it, and quietly shut it for the last time. A chapter of my life had just closed.

As I drove away that night, I wasn't alone. Jesus was there, and once again, His grace had seen me through.

26

God's Provision

I was so relieved after finalizing everything with the house in Idaho and having the move behind me. A weight had been lifted off my shoulders, and I returned to Montana with a considerably lighter load.

Life continued on, and little by little, I felt joy coming back into my world. I was able to laugh with the children and smile at something cute they said or did.

Although some days went well and I felt strong and confident, there were still days when everything fell apart around me. During those times, God's hand is often seen so clearly. He knows when we are at our lowest point and comes in like a knight in shining armor to save the day. His grace carries us through our trial, and when it's over and the dust settles, we think back on it and wonder at His majesty. We see so clearly that He was there holding, sustaining, and providing. And once again, we are reminded that we are not alone.

One of those disaster days began about the same as the day before—nothing special. One moment led into another until the day was in full swing. I loaded the children into Jacob's truck and headed off to do a few errands. I don't remember why I chose to drive the truck that day instead of our minivan. Perhaps it was because I sometimes felt closer to Jacob in the vehicle he had been so fond of.

The afternoon shadows were lengthening by the time I returned home, turned into our driveway, and pushed the garage door opener. I slowly pulled the truck into the garage and cut the engine. The boys were out of their seatbelts in a flash, racing to get out of the truck. Clayton was in the front passenger seat, and Caleb was in the seat directly behind him. The truck doors are double doors, and the back door can't open until the person in the front seat opens his door first. Clayton swung his door open and was rising up out of his seat, preparing to jump down. Meanwhile, Caleb had thrust his door open and managed to hop from the truck before his little brother.

I was busy unbuckling Lydia from her car seat on the driver's side when I looked up just in time to see Clayton take a nosedive out of the vehicle. It occurred so quickly that I wasn't sure what had happened except I knew Clayton was in serious trouble. He had fallen face first from the seat of the truck onto the concrete floor.

I quickly dashed around to his side. Thoughts flashed through my mind at the speed of light. What would I find on the other side of the truck? How much blood would there be? How many teeth would be missing? And what in the world had happened anyway? How had he lost his balance?

I rounded the back corner of the truck just in time to see Clayton trying to pick himself up. A sob was caught in the back of his throat, trying to make its way out. His face was ashen, and his mouth was full of blood.

Scooping him up in my arms, I held him as his breath came back. Screams filled the garage and bounced from one wall to the other. I ran inside to the closest bathroom, grabbed a washcloth, and ran cool water over it. I put it over his mouth and cradled him as I rocked back and forth, trying to soothe his pain. My first goal was to calm him before I inspected the damage.

I was afraid to pull the washcloth away. What was I going to find? With that much blood, I knew it couldn't be good. My heart was pounding, but I remained calm.

Eventually, Clayton quieted to a mere whimper and then stopped crying altogether. I prepared myself for the worst and slowly pulled away the washcloth. There was still a lot of blood, but I could see that only one tooth had been damaged. The top right tooth was hanging by a thread, loose enough that it would need to come out and yet tight enough that it wasn't going to fall out on its own. He needed to see a dentist and have it pulled. Fortunately, it was only a baby tooth and another one would grow back in time.

Meanwhile, Clayton needed help. His lips were cut and swollen, his gums were bloody, and his tooth was hanging. I was thankful things weren't worse. Still, my heart sank. I didn't have insurance for the kids, and we didn't have a regular dentist there in town. What was I going to do? I carried Clayton to the couch and made him as comfortable as I could. I grabbed the phone book and began calling dentist after dentist, trying to find someone to help.

Much to my dismay, I soon discovered that most dentist offices were closed on Fridays, and on this particular Friday, the other half that may have been open were at a dentists' convention in another town. I was failing to find anyone open and able to help my son.

I love how Jesus works. He knows exactly what we need and who to direct us to. Finally, I found a dentist with an emergency phone number listed. I tried it, and within a few seconds I heard, "Hello?"

"Yes," I quickly said and then began pouring out my story to this off-duty dentist. I felt so bad interrupting his day, but I was desperate to help my son. The man on the other end listened and then kindly responded, "Well, I am out in the field right now on my farm, but bring him into my office, and I will come have a look at him."

"Oh, thank you so much!" I said, my heart singing with relief. I quickly wrote down the directions to his office and hung up the phone. I gathered the troop and piled them all in the truck. There was no time to switch car seats into the minivan. By this time, the bleeding had stopped, and Clayton was completely calm as he held the cloth over his mouth. It was more for security than anything.

Thankfully, the dentist office was not far. After I pulled in, the dentist arrived only moments later. I unloaded the kids and instructed them to be on their best behavior. The office was dark since everyone had the day off. Go figure, this happened to be carpet cleaning day too, so all the furniture had been moved. Now I really felt bad trekking across their freshly cleaned floors with my group.

But Dr. Dalen didn't seem to mind. He flicked on the lights and had Clayton up in the examination chair in no time. He slapped his gloves on and went right to work. After a good look, he said, "He needs to see an oral surgeon." Turns out that the extent of the damage was not something the dentist was comfortable dealing with. Clayton not only needed his tooth pulled but stitches as well.

Again, my heart sank. Where in the world was I going to find an oral surgeon?

Dr. Dalen then said, "I'll call an oral surgeon for you."

I was so relieved and thankful. Within a matter of minutes, I was back out the door and in the car with an appointment scheduled. And that kind man never charged me a dime.

I had no idea how long this next appointment would last or how involved it would be, so I called my mom to see if she would watch the other children for me. She agreed, we made the switch, and Clayton and I were soon on our way. I finally relaxed a bit knowing my son would soon be taken care of. He wouldn't have to spend the weekend with a tooth hanging, waiting for an opening next week. I couldn't be more grateful.

We arrived at the oral surgeon's office and were escorted into a room. Clayton was a brave little man as they laid him out and began the examination. I sat nearby watching and wondering how much all this was going to cost. I wasn't familiar with an oral surgeon's charges, but I expected it to be a fair amount.

Dr. Weber soon finished his inspection and explained his next step. Besides the loose tooth, there were multiple lacerations on Clayton's lips and gums. After Dr. Weber pulled the tooth, he would stitch Clayton back together.

With a few chuckles and cheers about how brave Clayton was, the surgeon and his assistant set to work, fixing his mouth. I appreciated their kindness. Their cheerful attitude and gentle gestures soothed my son—and me too, for that matter.

Before long, the procedure was over, and Clayton was free to go.

They sent me home with a list of instructions and told me to bring him back in about a week to remove the stitches. I thanked them and headed back to the car. Words can't describe my relief. God had seen me through. He had worked everything out perfectly.

Going through something like this is hard enough when your husband is at home waiting to wrap you in his arms. But it's even more difficult when his arms are no longer there. Even in this, God sees, cares, and understands.

I pulled into my driveway. My tired mind and body needed rest, and my heart needed comfort. As I drove into the garage, I noticed a bouquet of flowers. I retrieved them and read the attached card. They were from Jacob!

A family friend who had no idea of what had transpired that day felt led to drop them off to me as if Jacob himself had sent them. I was blown away. It was as if Jesus was letting me have that hug I needed so much. He was letting me know Jacob still loved me but even more that He did too. God's love will never fail, nor will He ever cease providing for my every need. His grace is there for the long haul through thick and thin to cover any situation in my life.

And do you know, that oral surgeon never charged me a dime? Sometimes the goodness of Jesus is simply too much for words.

27

Overcome Those Summer Blues

Summer was in full swing. Golden sunbeams sparkled on the lake behind our house. The now snowless mountains towered in the background and made quite a contrast against the blue sky. It was a treat for me to slip out to our back deck with a cup of coffee and sit there in the sunshine. The warmth of the sun not only soothed my physical body, it somehow managed to warm my heart as well.

However, with the coming of summer, I felt a new emotion awakening. Summer is a time when families are supposed to get out and make memories together. It is a time to go on vacation, go swimming, grill hot dogs, and watch fireworks on the Fourth of July. The longing for my husband was almost more than I could handle. I ached to be able to do those things with him again. I knew one day in heaven we would, but that seemed so far away. Who knows how many years I'd have to wait? I needed him now! But that would never be.

I pushed past the loneliness in my heart and made a decision that influenced the course of the summer. Jacob was a man of adventure and discovery. There was no way he would want his wife to sit around and mourn all summer long and keep his kids from getting out and having a few experiences of their own. So with great determination, I resolved to follow the prompting in my heart and make this summer one to remember. I don't know if God gives reports about people on Earth to their family members in heaven, but if so, I hoped God would include the adventures of this summer. I wanted Jacob to smile and say, "That's my girl."

My rental was normally used as a vacation home for people seeking adventure in Montana. Skiing, fishing, hunting, hiking, biking—you name it; it's out there, just waiting to be enjoyed. At least that's what the covers of the tourist magazines all portrayed. There were several sitting around the coffee table at my house, so I picked one up to see what wild exploits I could find to do with the children that summer. I was thinking big ... a hot air balloon ride or maybe even a helicopter tour! I was quickly brought back to reality when I found out how much those activities cost. I set my sights a little more realistically and decided to explore the free stuff.

Glacier National Park wasn't far from our house and offered a variety of free activities. This would be perfect. I bought a season pass and was at liberty to enter any time I wanted at no additional cost. Lake McDonald lay at the entrance to the park. Nestled on its shores was a small tourist village where one could eat, sleep, shop for souvenirs, and, of course, taste some of Montana's delicious huckleberry ice cream.

Farther into the park were several other lodges, restaurants, and shops, but other than that, it was nothing but beautiful wilderness filled with bubbling brooks, wildflowers, cedar trees, rocky cliffs, and great hiking trails. This was the kind of adventure I was looking for.

I decided it wise to keep my ambition in balance and stick to the well-traveled trails. A single mom with four small children doesn't need to become the next headline on the front page of the newspaper: MISSING IN ACTION or SNACK FOR HUNGRY BEAR. Nonetheless, I wasn't going to let the fact that I was alone with four kids keep us from adventure.

It was time to move on and see the color of life once again. I had to stay busy and focus on God's call for my life—raising these precious little ones for His glory. I would teach them how to press on despite the sorrow of the heart that makes one want to close up and hide forever. Together we would make joyful memories again.

Our first hike that summer was a delightful boardwalk through a cedar forest. Its level pathway made it especially charming and child friendly. There were no steep inclines or drastic declines to meander up and down. The forest was cool under the shade of the towering cedars above. Sunlight filtered through the boughs and danced on the wooded floor as the gentle breeze caused the branches to sway back and forth. Sounds of the children's laughter filled the air and bounced from trunk to trunk as they skipped along the path.

For our second hike, I decided to move us up a notch from beginner to intermediate. I packed lots of snacks and water and divided them into two backpacks. I would carry one along with baby Lydia, and the boys would take turns carrying the other one. We loaded up and headed out.

When we arrived, the parking lot was completely full. Normally, this wouldn't be much of an issue on a family outing. Dad would simply let the family out at the trailhead, take the car down the road a spell until he found a sufficient place to park, and then jog back to rejoin the family. But we weren't a normal family anymore, and since I was the only driver, this plan obviously wouldn't work. I couldn't drop the kids off by themselves, and I wasn't about to give up and go home simply because I couldn't find a parking spot.

I drove down the road until I found an adequate place to park along the side of the road. Even though it was the first available spot, it was still pretty far from the trail. It looked like the kids and I were going to have a hike before our hike. We piled out of the car and walked single file down the side of the road and up toward the main parking lot.

We eventually reached our destination, took a quick bathroom break, and headed for the path. Our objective this time was a high mountain lake at the end of the trail ... a trail that went up! As we began, I took a long look at the steep route ahead of us and the sign posted next to it that read, "GRIZZLY BEAR COUNRY." *Hmmm ...*

But once again, I wasn't going to give up. The trail looked steep now but would surely level out at some point. And the bears ... well, there were a lot of people on the path that day to give them enough variety to choose from. Certainly we wouldn't be the first pick for the platter. With determination and a slight shift of my backpack, we continued on.

We proved to be the spectacle on the trail that day. Almost every one we passed had something to say. Usually, it came out something like, "Wow, you sure are brave to make this trek alone with four little ones!"

At first, I thought nothing of it, but as the trail continued on and on and Lydia grew heavier and heavier, I muttered to myself, "You're not brave, you're nuts! Completely crazy!"

I must say the view around us was beautiful, though. We needed to make it to the top. No turning back now. So despite the kids' tired legs and my aching back, we pushed on. Here and there we stopped for a snack and water break. Near the end, several hikers making their descent encouraged us on with "It's not far. You'll be there soon."

No one on the trail that day was more joyful to see the top than we were. As soon as we could see water through the trees, we cheered. We reached the water's edge and plopped our packs down in relief. The lake was calm, cool, and beautiful. Chipmunks scurried around our feet, begging for a snack. My back and shoulders were screaming in agony from carrying Lydia for so long. I scooped her out of the pack and let her walk around as the older children played. Everyone was happy to have made it.

It was a very exhausted group of five that finally made it back down to the bottom that day. We were pretty much wiped out as we loaded up and drove off. The kids were troopers for sure, brave and strong. Their daddy would have been so proud.

I'll never forget the impact that summer had on healing my heart and our family. Getting out again and living the adventure of life was soothing. With God's strength, I carried on and lived another day and another. God had given me the determination to keep living life. It would be a one-day-at-a-time journey, but His grace would see me through.

28

All for His Glory

At some point in life, we are all hounded by the age-old question, "What is my purpose on this earth?" Why is this? I think for those who haven't yet opened their hearts to Jesus Christ as Savior, it's the voice of God calling to them. He is drawing their hearts to Him with this question. He wants them to seek the answer because the answer will only be found in Him. It can't be found in people, things, or ideas.

This gnawing question may abate for a time, but it will always resurface. Some will settle and simply choose to live with this thorn in their side. They'll spend the rest of their lives without the peace and fulfillment that only Jesus can bring. But some will finally listen to that inward call and reach for the answer in God. Peace and complete fulfillment will fill their soul, and that gnawing question will subside ... for a time anyway.

This leads me to the second conclusion of my original question. Those of us who have already received Christ as Savior have found the answer to our heart-throbbing question. We are here to live for Jesus in everything we do and say. Our hearts are at rest knowing we have tremendous purpose in life. And yet sometimes we still hear those words playing over and over in our minds. That age-old question often resurfaces when we're going through a trial or heartbreak, taunting us when we are weak and vulnerable. But this time it's not the voice of God stirring us to find hope and fulfillment in Him alone. It's the voice of our greatest enemy of all time, Satan, whispering the question as he challenges the peace we've found in Jesus. He seeks us in our weakness and tempts us to doubt God's promise to us. He may even bring it to another level and change it from "What is my purpose on Earth?" to "I have *no* purpose on Earth."

Just because we have given our lives into the hands of Jesus doesn't mean Satan has given up on us. Nothing delights him more than trying to discourage one of God's own. His anger burns toward Jesus and the freedom people find in Him. Satan wants to keep people bound in their chains of sin and guilt. Once they have been set free, he has lost his ownership of them; however, he still tries his best to dampen their spirits and rob them of their joy.

First Peter 5:8 warns us, "Be sober, be vigilant; because your adversary the devil, as a roaring lion, walketh about, seeking whom he may devour." That cunning lion liked stalking me during my days of loneliness and grief. He roared discouragement any time he had the chance in order to weaken my trust in God. A couple of days in particular I thought to myself, *What in the world are you doing, Dawn? Look at you. It's just the kids and you out in the woods of Montana. Think of all your friends who have so much going for them in their lives. They're thriving in the great calling God has for them by doing something important for the kingdom of God and His glory! And look at you ... just a single mom. One of your worst nightmares. What good can you do?*

During these attacks, it is vitally important to act quickly. In our own strength we are no match to resist Satan's lies and taunts and will easily succumb to despondency. We have to run to Jesus, and the sooner the better. The longer we linger, trying to fight the attack on our own, the weaker we'll become. Jesus is our only hope.

In these times of discouragement, I slipped off by myself (as by myself as I could with four children in the house), fell on my knees, and planted my face in the rug. I then poured everything out to Jesus.

I realized He already knew every square inch of my heart and mind, but He wanted to hear it from me. He longed for me to tell Him all that was troubling my heart. Psalm 34:15 says, "The eyes of the LORD are upon the righteous, and His ears are open unto their cry."

Jesus is never too busy for us, nor does he ever turn us away. We come to Him a dozen times a day concerning the same thing, and He will always be there to hold us and listen to our cry. He will never say, "Goodness sakes, my child, you told Me that five minutes ago. We already talked that one over."

Instead, He will gently whisper encouragement into our hearts, maybe through a thought, the lyrics of a song, or a Bible verse. He will meet us at our point of weakness and give us His strength to resist the taunts from our enemy who lurks about.

I pictured my life as a jigsaw puzzle. All I could see were the pieces in disarray, scattered across the table. Nothing made sense to me and looked like a purposeless mess. I didn't even have the picture on the box as a reference to put my life together. But you see, Jesus has this amazing ability (because He is God) to see the end result before it even exists. He sees the beautiful picture the puzzle will one day become. The trick is in letting Him put the pieces together. It's not my job to help Him. I'll only mess things up. My job is simply to trust that He knows what He is doing, and that's all that matters.

He also opened my eyes to something I already knew but had allowed Satan to tell me was unimportant. I do have a calling on my life. I am living with a great purpose. Jesus has called me to be the mother to Caleb, Clayton, Lacey, and Lydia Cole. It may seem insignificant in the eyes of some, but no calling of God is unimportant in His eyes. No matter how big or small, trivial or grandiose it may seem to us, if God has called us to it, nothing is more important.

My brother-in-law once told me that fulfilling God's call on our lives is found in abiding in the center of His will for us that day. His words made me stop and think. Sometimes we seek after what we consider a grand calling from God and miss the whole point. By doing this, we abandon what He meant for us to do in order to find what we think He wants us to do or accomplish for His glory. We must remember that everything we do in our day-to-day lives can be for His glory. "Whether therefore ye eat, or drink, or whatsoever ye do, do all to the glory of God" (1 Corinthians 10:31).

I'm not saying we can't ever dream to do great things or to step from one job to another. Quite the contrary. Jesus often moves us from one thing to another and then another. He has great plans for each one of us. But He does it according to His will and timetable. What we must remember is to be content with where He has placed us here and now. For the time being, this is exactly where He wants us, and there is absolutely nothing more noble we could be doing than living each moment in the center of His will.

In my kitchen window, I have a piece of paper that contains one simple sentence that says, "I am alive to live for You." I heard it in a song one day (Holding Nothing Back by Tim Hughes) on the Christian radio station, and inspired, I jotted it down as a daily reminder of my purpose on this earth. Every second, minute, hour, day, week, and year I live in this life should be for one reason: Jesus. And whatever He brings or allows to come into each day should be viewed as an opportunity for His glory to shine through me (Romans 8:28).

29

Just Jesus and Me

Some of my most painful yet most beautiful times came in the evening after the children were in bed and the house was silent. Before Jacob died, those few hours each night were such a treat. With the kids in bed and the dishes done, it was our time to be alone together. But now he was gone, and the house was more silent than ever. I always felt his absence, but especially during those quiet moments alone.

My heart ached for my husband. I wanted more than anything to be able to run into his arms and pour out my heart to him. I wanted to tell him about my day, to share the ups and downs. He was supposed to be here laughing with me about the cute things the kids said or did and encouraging me on the days they misbehaved.

Every night I went upstairs to an empty bedroom. He wasn't there. His arms weren't waiting to hold me close. The loneliness was indescribable. But looking back on those moments, I find they were endearing. You are shocked, I am sure. Let me explain.

Those moments were "Jesus and me" time. Every evening, I fell on my knees next to my bed in my empty room and often spent a long while there in prayer. Of course I prayed for the kids and myself, but I also, and probably more importantly, began praying for the needs of others. Reaching beyond my pain into someone else's world did my heart good.

Some evenings I listened to a sermon online or read my Bible. But the evenings I look back on with the fondest memories were the ones when I was completely exhausted from a full day of being both dad and mom. My body was weary to the bone, my brain completely fatigued, and my heart utterly broken. I had no strength left in me except to flop on my bed in front of my computer. In those times, music best soothed my weary soul. I would click on my favorite worship songs and lay my head down on the blankets. As the music played, Jesus reached for my heart and encircled it with His love. As He held me close, His strength filled my soul.

My body would then begin to relax. Sometimes I fell asleep this way. Other times, I remained awake and yet completely at peace. I'm not trying to paint the picture that my pain instantly vanished, and that I was suddenly sorrow free. Not so. My heart still ached, and I still felt weary. There were times when I wished Jesus would appear to me in person. I longed to physically crawl up on His lap and have Him wrap His arms around me as I cried. And by God's amazing power, I felt His presence there with me. Even though I couldn't see Him, He was there, loving me, cradling me, strengthening me.

I certainly wouldn't have volunteered to walk this path in life, to lose my husband and endure such extreme heartache. But through it, I was seeing the amazing beauty of Jesus Christ as never before. I felt God's love and tenderness in such an awesome way that it melted my heart. He hadn't left me alone to aimlessly walk through this valley but was right by my side every moment of every day. My love for Him began to deepen and flourish.

Someday, after my life on this earth has passed, I'll finally be able to see Jesus face-to-face. I've already dreamed of that day and what it may be like. I imagine I'll come before His throne completely awestruck by the glory all around me and fall on my face before Him. He will then come to me and lift me into His arms. I'll wrap my arms around Him, hold Him close, and whisper, "Thank You ... thank You ... thank You for all You have done for me."

It will be a magnificent day beyond my wildest dreams, but until then, I know beyond a shadow of a doubt that Jesus will always be with me in spirit. Every day for the rest of my life, He will remain faithful and true. He will be the love of my heart and I of His.

For any of you who may be facing an extremely difficult time in your life, run to Jesus. He will be there for you. Don't expect everything to miraculously change or all your troubles to disappear. Jesus is definitely capable of this, but often He allows our trial to remain to build our faith in and dependency on Him. It's painful becoming stronger in heart and spirit. It doesn't come without a cost. But He will remain faithful to you.

Don't block Him out or shove Him aside, thinking you can handle it on your own. You need Him. He's as close as a whisper away. Talk to Him, and tell Him how you hurt. You won't truly heal and become strong again without Him. Take the time to have some "Jesus and you" time. Don't put it off. He loves you more than you can fathom, and as you seek Him, you will feel His love in a deeper way. And I daresay your heart will fall deeper in love with Him too.

30

Jesus, My Forever Strength

Summer had passed, and autumn was in the air. The leaves on the trees began changing color from summer green to harvest gold. As I observed the changing of the season, I felt a stirring inside. I knew the time was drawing near. I'd almost been a widow for a whole year.

I could barely fathom it. My emotions were jumbled. Part of me could hardly believe it had been that long, and the other part could barely comprehend that it hadn't been longer. Soon I wouldn't be able to say, "A year ago Jacob was still here." The more time went by, the larger the gap became when we were last together. Somehow it hurt more when I thought of it this way. However, if I flipped it around, each day that passed drew us one day closer to being together again in heaven. This thought was helpful unless I allowed myself to wonder how many days there might be. More than likely, many more days remained than what I hoped. I told myself to take one day at a time and to not think too far ahead. Jesus would be here for me today, and if He gave me tomorrow, He'd be there too, and so on and so forth until the end of my days.

I also realized I needed to rely on His strength to carry me through each day. A special friend of mine who had lost his young wife to the same vicious cancer as my husband's encouraged me in this, and I've never forgotten it. His need for Jesus was as great as mine, for he, too, had young children.

When I was really struggling one day and told him how I felt, he responded, "The worst thing I can do is try to rely on my own strength when I know it's only God's strength that will pull me through." His words echoed in my mind like sound waves from a giant gong. They weren't new to me, but sometimes we need lots of reminders about things we already know. I realized that on days when I'd been particularly frustrated and impatient, I was relying on my own strength.

During the immediate months after Jacob's death, I felt extremely weak. I rarely made it past my morning shower without asking God for His strength and grace to fill me and help me make it through the day. But as time when on and I became stronger, there were mornings when I forgot to specifically ask Him to carry me through the day. In addition to these were the days when I started off on the right track by acknowledging my need for Him, but as the day progressed, the cares of life distracted and drew me into relying upon my own strength to make things happen.

Mike's words helped me realize how vital it is to always acknowledge my need for Jesus. I need Him on the days when everything is crumbling as well as on the days when everything is going well. In every situation, I need His strength to carry me.

Second Corinthians 12:9 is one of my favorite Bible verses. Here we find the apostle Paul pleading with Jesus to remove a particular infirmity that plagued him, which Paul refers to as a "thorn in the flesh." Jesus responds, "My grace is sufficient for thee: for My strength is made perfect in weakness." In other words, Jesus is saying, "No, Paul, I won't remove it from you, but I will give you My grace and strength to bear it. Through your trial, My strength will be made perfect in you."

It didn't take Paul long to submit to God's will as he replies, "...Most gladly therefore will I rather glory in my infirmities, that the power of Christ may rest upon me. Therefore I take pleasure in infirmities, in reproaches, in necessities, in persecutions, in distresses for Christ's sake: for when I am weak, then am I strong" (2 Corinthians 12:9-10).

How beautiful that Jesus can be seen in our weakness. When we feel at our lowest point, the power of God Almighty rests upon us. When we are weak and fragile, He is strong in us. When you stop and ponder this, it can be mind blowing. The One who spoke light into existence, hung each star in place, and created each towering mountain and tiny flower is the One who promises to fill us with His power. No wonder Paul decided he would "glory"—no wait—he said, "take pleasure in" hardships. He saw the bigger picture and decided it was worth it.

I wonder how often we miss seeing God's power at work in us because we decide we can handle it ourselves. May we be more like Paul and glory even in our hardships. And as we acknowledge our need for Jesus, may we feel, see, and know God's majesty at work in us.

31

Choosing to Trust

About a week before the first anniversary of Jacob's death, I was alone in the house. The kids had gone to spend the night at my parents' as they did every Sunday night, which gave me an opportunity each week to catch my breath and unwind. I always looked forward to my "Mommy Time."

I treated myself to a movie that night. It was one of those girly/romantic movies I used to enjoy but had lost taste for since Jacob's death. However, as time slowly passed and my heart gradually healed, I felt the interest begin to bloom again—maybe more than I was really ready for. Sure enough, the movie was sweet and romantic and triggered something deep inside. As soon as it was over, I lost it.

The wonder of being in love was more than I could handle. I can't even begin to put into words the splendor of truly loving someone and having them truly love you in return. It is an amazing thing, and I missed it so much.

I fell to my bedroom floor as heavy sobs shook my body. The pain was so intense that I could barely breathe. I agonized over my life and what had befallen me. At first my tears came from a heart full of sorrow. I missed Jacob with every fiber of my being and longed for him back. I wanted to hold him close and feel his arms holding me.

After awhile, though, my tears turned from sad to angry. Losing my dream, especially when I'd held it within my very grasp, was so unfair! Jacob had been my dream come true, and the life we shared was amazing and wonderful. We were so in love, soul mates in every way. But now he was gone. I had done everything in my power to keep him here with me, but no matter how hard I tried, I couldn't do it.

I struggled to hold onto my dream as one holds a handful of sand. No matter how hard you try, that sand soon slips through your fingers and is gone. I had it all, and now it was all gone. The pain of that reality shook me.

Eventually, the tears of anger turned back into torrents of sorrow again. I screamed in agony to the four walls in my room. I cried out every thought that entered my mind to God. Not that He needed me to raise my voice in order to hear, but I needed to release my pain verbally and *loud*.

At long last, I grew silent. My strength was gone, and all my tears had been cried out (at least for the moment). I lay there one sloppy mess, heartbroken to the core. I glanced up at a picture of Jacob and me, and in the quietness of my heart, I began a silent conversation with the Lord. I envisioned Him saying:

"Dawn, are you going to keep trusting Me?"

"Lord, you know I trust You," I thought to myself.

"You must choose to keep on trusting Me even though you can't understand my ways. Don't give up. Just keep trusting Me."

That night was a turning point in my heart. Jesus showed me I needed to let go of the dreams I had for my life. Even though Jacob was gone and wasn't coming back, I was still holding onto him in a selfish way. He was mine, and I hadn't been ready to let him go. I hadn't even been asked permission; he was simply taken away.

But our lives are not ours. As Christians, we belong to Jesus Christ. Jacob first and foremost belonged to the Lord. He had fulfilled his calling upon this earth; it had been his time to go. The "why" of it all wasn't for me to figure out. I was simply to believe that Jesus had a plan. The choice was up to me. Would I become angry or release my heart to Jesus and trust Him?

Jesus hadn't once forsaken me; I couldn't forsake Him now. I'd only been at this widow thing for a year. I didn't know what my future held, but I did know that the One who holds my future is faithful and true. Throughout the years, God has given me the grace to face every situation He allowed into my life. During Jacob's illness and this past year of widowhood, His portion increased, and I was confident it would always be that way.

As I picked myself off the floor that night, I believed that Jesus truly did care about my heart and my dreams. He had given me an amazing man to love and hold for eight years and had blessed us with four beautiful children. Yes, my plans had been altered, but God's hadn't. Jesus wasn't finished with me yet. I was on the right track with Him.

I believe with all my soul that He still has great plans for the children and me. I don't know what they will entail, but that's not my business. He will bring them to pass in His time and way. May Jesus grant me the grace to trust Him every step of the way. He will always be there holding me, loving me, and sustaining me. He will never let me go.

Jacob's legacy and his love for Jesus will continue on in our hearts. He will constantly be a part of us, and for as long as God gives us breath, we will carry on. May our lives and testimony of God's goodness bring Him honor and glory. One day, we will join Jacob in our heavenly home, and together we will thank Jesus for His amazing grace and for teaching us to find His strength in our weakness.

32

When Thunder Rolls

Sooner or later, all of us will face a difficult season in life when thunder begins to roll. Some storms are more severe than others and involve different degrees of pain, fear, grief, or depression. Some quickly blow in with a mighty gust, whip us around, and are gone, and we are left barely standing as we stare at the havoc around us. Day after day, we try picking up the pieces the best we can, but after awhile, it becomes too much to bear.

Then there are the storms we see coming on the distant horizon. The sky darkens as clouds build. The wind picks up, lightening streaks across the sky, and the low rumble of thunder slowly draws closer and louder. We brace ourselves as the storm hits. Day after day it rages, and instead of dying down, it only increases in intensity. We bravely struggle on, but after awhile, fatigue sets in.

So what do we do? There's no way to avoid the storms of life. They will come (John 16:33), so how can we survive them? I'd like to share with you a few things Jesus has shown me during my times of trial. I realize everyone has a different experience and learns different lessons, but we can encourage one another by sharing what we've learned.

When You Begin Doubting God's Ability

Predators, such as wolves and lions, like to stalk the weak and sickly. Attacking something that won't put up much of a fight is an easy kill. Satan is no dummy either. Someone who is weary and discouraged is an easy target and may have more of an open mind to what he has to say.

You have probably experienced this when you were at your lowest low, and Satan made a house call. After giving you a piece of his mind, he left you mulling over his discouraging thoughts—the biggest one being whether you should trust God any more.

I experienced this recently. I was sitting in my living room, thinking about all the difficulties in my life and all the prayers waiting to be answered. Sure enough, the doorbell rang (1 Peter 5:8–9). Satan is persistent, so when we don't open the door, he will try the window because he knows we will still hear him through the glass.

My mind replayed his lies. But you see, we Christians haven't been left weaponless (Ephesians 6:10–17). Among our weapons is the sword—God's amazing Word, the Bible.

> For the word of God is quick, and powerful, and sharper than any twoedged sword, piercing even to the dividing assunder of soul and spirit, and of the joints and marrow, and is a discerner of the thoughts and intents of the heart (Hebrews 4:12).

> And take the helmet of salvation, and the sword of the Spirit, which is the word of God (Ephesians 6:17).

This is the time that "sword" needs to come out. Slash it around for all its worth. Open your Bible and begin reading or quote portions from memory. Allow your mind to drift into the richness of God's Word. You'll find power there. There's no higher authority in heaven or on Earth than the Word of God. That's a pretty incredible thought—think on that for a while. Satan is no match against such power and will have no choice but to leave.

One of my favorite ways of "sword" fighting Satan is going over God's track record with him. He doesn't last long—in fact, rarely long enough for me to finish—but I continue anyway, basking in the glory of God.

This is the approach I used on that particular day:

Let's see ... Genesis 1:3, 14–16 tells us that in the beginning of time God spoke light into existence.

> And God said, "Let there be light": and there was light ... And God said, "Let there be lights in the firmament of the heaven to divide the day from the night; and let them be for signs, and for seasons, and for days, and years: And let them be for lights in the firmament of the heaven to give light upon the earth": and it was so. And God made two great lights; the greater light to rule the day, and the lesser light to rule the night: He made the stars also.

One second it was pitch black, and the very next there was light. That great ball of fire we call the sun came from a mere command of God. That's pretty incredible! Come on; think about it. The sun is enormous. Over one million earths could fit inside the sun. Picture a huge gumball machine filled with one million gumballs. We're nothing but a gumball compared to the sun. Pretty tiny, right? Oh, and we would need to blast one hundred billion tons of dynamite per second to match the energy the sun produces per second. The sun is one massive power that derived from the power of God. What a mighty Creator we have!

Satan's lies instantly diminished when I compared them to such supreme authority.

I continued:

If that's not convincing enough or you just want to hear more, let's proceed to the book of Exodus. When was the last time you thought about the Israelites crossing the Red Sea (Exodus 14:13–14, 21–31)?

> And Moses said unto the people, "Fear ye not, stand still, and see the salvation of the LORD, which He will shew to you to

day: for the Egyptians whom ye have seen today, ye shall see them again no more forever. The LORD shall fight for you, and ye shall hold your peace."

And Moses stretched out his hand over the sea; and the LORD caused the sea to go back by a strong east wind all that night, and made the sea dry land, and the waters were divided. And the children of Israel went into the midst of the sea upon the dry ground: and the waters were a wall unto them on their right hand, and on their left. And the Egyptians pursued, and went in after them into the midst of the sea, even all Pharaoh's horses, his chariots, and his horsemen.

And it came to pass, that in the morning watch the LORD looked unto the host of the Egyptians through the pillar of fire and of the cloud, and troubled the host of the Egyptians, And He took off their chariot wheels, that they drave them heavily: so that the Egyptians said, "Let us flee from the face of Israel; for the LORD fighteth for them against the Egyptians."

And the LORD said unto Moses, "Stretch out thine hand over the sea, that the waters may come again upon the Egyptians, upon their chariots, and upon their horsemen." And Moses stretched forth his hand over the sea, and the sea returned to his strength when the morning appeared; and the Egyptians fled against it; and the LORD overthrew the Egyptians in the midst of the sea. And the waters returned, and covered the chariots, and the horsemen, and all the host of Pharaoh that came into the sea after them; there remained not so much as one of them. But the children of Israel walked upon dry land in the midst of the sea; and the waters were a wall unto them on their right hand and on their left.

Thus the LORD saved Israel that day out of the hand of the Egyptians; and Israel saw the Egyptians dead upon the sea shore. And Israel saw that great work which the LORD did upon the Egyptians: and the people feared the LORD, and believed the LORD, and his servant Moses.

Most of us have heard this story before, but have you ever put on your imagination cap and placed your feet in the sandals of one of the Israelites that day? Let's try:

Okay, so you and two million others are pretty much scared out of your wits (Exodus 14:10). Any joy of finally making it out of that tiresome desert and to the Red Sea is completely gone as you hear Pharaoh's army marching after you. You left Egypt and came all this way to be slaughtered on the beach? Fear is mounting, threatening sheer panic.

Eventually, news spreads that Moses says not to fear because God is going to take care of everything. You wonder what in the world God has in mind because there sure are not many hiding places for two million people on this beach.

All of a sudden, a strong wind comes from nowhere. Darkness begins to fall as word reaches you of God's plan of escape. In the darkening shadows, you begin making out the formations of giant walls of water in the distant sea. An awestruck hum fills the air.

Okay, if you aren't already in awe, now would be a good time to be. Here you are, approaching the water's edge. Instead of the typical small waves that lap the shoreline, there are two towering walls of water on each side of you. In complete amazement, you take your first step and then the next, right out into the middle of the sea.

"What? ... Wow! ... Oh, my goodness!" You can barely contain your emotions. The walls of water to your right and left tower over you. No power known to man could ever hold back this much water. Your knees begin feeling a little weak at the awesomeness of almighty God, and a wave of reverence sweeps over you.

All night long, God holds back the Red Sea as all two million people pass through. Dawn breaks as the last few cross over. Eventually, you, too, reach the other side and take your first step out of the seabed and onto the beach. Relief surges through you only to turn to panic as you see the Egyptian army following in hot pursuit. At that time, Moses lifts his hand toward the sea, and the water begins falling on the Egyptians. All God had to do was remove his pinky finger that held back those enormous walls of water and ... well, you can imagine what happened next. As the water collided, I say it must have been a pretty majestic sight—maybe it even shook the ground a little. The sound must have been deafening.

The Bible is full of events like these that display the awesomeness of our God. I could have spent all day in my living room going over more just like them. But these were all it took to fill my heart once again with renewed faith to keep believing and trusting. The same God who spoke light out of His mouth and held back the flow of a mighty sea could certainly handle the issues in my life. Satan had lost this battle. The "sword" had triumphed over his lies.

Make Time for Jesus

Now it came to pass, as they went, that He entered into a certain village: and a certain woman named Martha received Him into her house. And she had a sister called Mary, which also sat at Jesus' feet, and heard His word. But Martha was cumbered about much serving, and came to Him, and said, "Lord, dost thou not care that my sister hath left me to serve alone? Bid her therefore that she help me."

And Jesus answered and said unto her, "Martha, Martha, thou art careful and troubled about many things: But one thing is needful: and Mary hath chosen that good part, which shall not be taken away from her" (Luke 10:38–42).

I'm sure most of you have heard this story before. The obvious lesson from this passage is that it's important to spend time with Jesus. But let's look a little deeper and consider this phrase, "Mary has chosen."

Spending time with Jesus is a choice. It's really that simple. Jesus didn't hound Martha and force her to sit down. He advised her what to do because He knew what was best for her, but He didn't yank her hand to make her sit. Our relationship with Christ should be one of love. When you love someone, you *want* to be with him or her. You desire to talk, laugh, cry—whatever. You just want to be together.

But, even in a loving relationship there are times when life becomes busy and we put off those we love. This isn't a good thing. We need to be aware of this and make the choice to stop. The same is true with Jesus. We love Him, and yet at times we become so wrapped up with "stuff," "worried and troubled about many things," as Jesus told Martha. Each person's list may look different but could include: daily chores, issues at work, the Christmas party at church, problems in the family, deep personal sorrow, lack of work, a school fundraiser, a garden to harvest, etc.

No matter what is going on in your life, you have to *choose* to take time for Jesus. Protect your relationship with Him. Guard it—it's precious. You need to be with Him; it's what keeps your relationship healthy and thriving. Jesus knew this and spent time in prayer with His Father (Matthew 14:23; Luke 6:12; 9:18).

Some of you may be thinking, "Now, don't put that guilt trip on me." That's not my intention. I only want to make God's heart known. Did you know He wants to be with you? God came to talk with Adam and Eve in the garden of Eden on a regular basis (Genesis 3:8) because He desired fellowship with them. He loved spending time with them just as He loves spending time with you.

Don't put Him off. Just like with Martha, God is not going to force you. He wants you to *choose* to be with Him. Put down the TV remote or the exciting new novel, wake up a little earlier, and let the dishes sit. Find some way to spend time with Him. It doesn't have to be hours. If you have that much time, wonderful, but don't burden yourself. You'll miss the point.

Just be with Him. Maybe play some worship music, sit down, lay your head back, and think about how amazing He is. Be still and know He is God (Psalm 46:10). You may have concerns to share with Him or requests to make ... He wants to hear them all (Matthew 7:7;

Luke 11:9; Philippians 4:6). Your heart is important to Him. He loves you more than you could ever comprehend. Let Him shower His love upon you. If you're hurting, He will comfort you. If you're lonely, He will be with you. If you're afraid, He will give you peace. As you diligently make time for Him, He will bless you. "But without faith it is impossible to please Him: for he that cometh to God must believe that He is, and that He is a rewarder of them that diligently seek Him" (Hebrews 11:6).

God Is Listening!

One day I was sitting in my little prayer spot (usually on the rug in my bathroom—weird spot, I know), when all of a sudden it hit me. "Jesus truly hears every word I am saying!"

Well, it's about time, you're thinking to yourself.

Okay, so I already understand this. But you know what it's like when something you've known for years suddenly becomes alive and vibrant in a brand-new way. That's how it was for me that day. I sat there with tears pouring down my face and gratitude and awe filling my heart.

Sometimes, it's easy to pray and forget that we are really talking to someone. We aren't talking to the wall; we are talking to an amazing God who is very much alive and hears every word we say. Jesus loves His kids, so you bet He's listening! "The eyes of the LORD are upon the righteous, and His ears are open unto their cry ... The righteous cry, and the LORD heareth, and delivereth them out of all their troubles" (Psalm 34:15, 17).

But what about when discouragement catches up with you? What about when you feel your prayers are unheard, that nothing has changed? Let's look at Luke 18:1–8:

> And He spake a parable unto them to this end, that men ought always to pray, and not to faint; Saying, "There was in a city a judge, which feared not God, neither regarded man: And there was a widow in that city; and she came unto him, saying, 'Avenge me of my adversary.' And he would not for a while:

but afterward he said within himself, 'Though I fear not God, nor regard man: Yet because this widow troubleth me, I will avenge her, lest by her continual coming she weary me.'"

And the Lord said, "Hear what the unjust judge saith. And shall not God avenge His own elect, which cry day and night unto Him, though He bear long with them? I tell you that He will avenge them speedily. Nevertheless, when the Son of Man cometh, shall He find faith on the earth?"

These are the verses I pull out when I'm feeling discouraged. Whether you are a widow or not, this story is for you. The purpose of this parable is clearly labeled in the opening verse. Jesus knew we would have times of weakness and would need specific encouragement.

If this judge who didn't care about this widow let alone love her answered her plea, how much more will our heavenly Father who does love us answer our cry? Keep in mind that it may take awhile; the passage does say, "Though He bears long with them." Don't panic if you've been praying for a while and nothing is happening. Something *is* happening, but *what* exactly? That is for God to know, not us.

One more very important thing to keep in mind is that God will answer but only according to His perfect will and not ours. "And this is the confidence that we have in Him, that, if we ask any thing according to His will, He heareth us: And if we know that He hears us, whatsoever we ask, we know that we have the petitions that we desired of Him" (1 John 5:14–15).

There's nothing wrong in telling Jesus all that's on your mind and how you'd love for Him to answer your prayer. He says to ask (Matthew 7:7–8). So please do. Your desires are important to Him, and He will answer. It just might be totally different from what you expect. So hold loosely to your plan because He may want to remodel it.

Sometimes our requests are answered exactly as we had hoped, and sometimes they aren't. But we can rest assured they will *always* be answered in the best way. We think we know what's best for the person we're praying for or for us, but we don't. God does.

So when the storms of life blow and Satan comes knocking, go over God's flawless track record with him. He won't last long, and in the meantime, your faith will be strengthened. Always make time for Jesus. No matter what, your faith needs to stay healthy and strong. God wants to love you and feel your love for Him as well. And never forget, He hears your every word and answers in the very best way because He sees all, knows all, and cares about you.

Thank you for coming with me on this journey. Just as Jesus has been with me every step of the way, He wants to be with you too. He wants to carry you and give you the strength you will need to make it. He wants to wipe your tears and hold you as you cry. He wants to heal your hurts and bring you joy again.

Have you given your life to Jesus? If so, what I've said has been a reminder of the priceless gift you have in Jesus. But if you haven't, I encourage you to give your life to Him, for without Him, we are lost in our sin, will never find true strength, peace, joy, or healing, and life after death will be a permanent separation from Him. Don't wait till then because it will be too late. Start celebrating life with Him here and now. The life He gives will never end.

In closing, let me leave you with a quote from my husband's journal:

> This day is not my own, it has been bought with the blood of Jesus Christ for my life by faith. I know that whatever comes into my life has been carefully sifted through the hands of a loving Father. Knowing this, I can walk boldly in obedience and believe that God will bring me through trials, joy, decisions, and peace—all to bring glory to His name as my faith is perfected.
> —February 18, 1999

No matter what you're facing right now, the deep hurt or impossible situation, remember it has already been sifted through the hands of Jesus Christ. Don't give up. He will bring you through because He loves you.

Epilogue:
The Cole Family (2012)

Wow... It has been three years since my Jacob died. It seems much longer ...

He is still smiling down on us from the photo on the wall, loving us all the way from heaven. It's still not the same without him, though. It hurts that there are no Jacob hugs, father-and-sons fishing trips, or daddy-and-daughter dates. He will always be missed.

However, I am pleased to say that the children and I are doing very well. Jesus has been my lifeline for sure. He's taken me through each step of my grieving process with tenderness and patience and has given me joy for mourning. But that doesn't mean everything is always rosy. Far from it. There are still tears, discouragements, frustrations, and loneliness, but He walks beside me every day and reminds me to trust Him. He helps me find peace in His presence. I am far from perfect and often fail miserably, but He lovingly picks me up and replaces my weakness with His strength. God has also provided a way for me to be a stay-at-home mom. I feel so blessed. I know it is what Jacob would have wanted.

Caleb, ten, is in fourth grade, and Clayton, eight, is in second grade. Both boys attend Stillwater Christian School and are doing very well. This is their first year in a school facility since I homeschooled them the previous years. They've adjusted well and absolutely love it.

Lacey, six, is in first grade. I am homeschooling her one more year and plan to send her to school with her brothers next fall. Lydia, three, has had the hardest time understanding why she can't "do" school like everyone else, but she is finally adjusting. I plan on spending this school year with my girls. Now that this book is completed, I hope to do some fun things with them, such as cooking, crafts, etc.

So as a whole, the children are doing very well. God has brought healing and has helped them deal with what has happened to our family.

After my decision to permanently stay in Montana, we built a house across the street from my parents, who are a great source of support for us. We still keep in close contact with Jacob's side of the family. Our ties with them have increased since Jacob's death. We are family and always will be.

I look forward to the plans God has for our future here on Earth and the even more amazing plans He has for us in heaven. If you need prayer or a listening ear, jot me a note. I'd enjoy hearing from you. dp.cole4@gmail.com

> For this cause I bow my knees unto the Father of our Lord Jesus Christ, of whom the whole family in heaven and earth is named, That He would grant you, according to the riches of His glory, to be strengthened with might by His Spirit in the inner man; That Christ may dwell in your hearts by faith; that ye, being rooted and grounded in love, may be able to comprehend with all the saints what is the breadth, and length, and depth, and height; And to know the love of Christ, which passeth knowledge, that ye might be filled with all the fullness of God.

> Now unto Him that is able to do exceedingly abundantly above all that we ask or think, according to the power that worketh in us, unto Him be glory in the church by Christ Jesus throughout all ages, world without end. Amen (Ephesians 3:14–21).

Photo Gallery

Bible College Days (2000)

Graduation Day (2000)

Our Wedding Day (August 31, 2001)

Dad and Sons on Ski Chairs (2006)

Jacob and Children at Josiah and Valoree's Wedding (2007)

Cole Family at the County Fair (2008)

Family Photo (2008)

Dad and Lacey, Mexico (2009)

Our Last Photo Together, Mexico (2009)

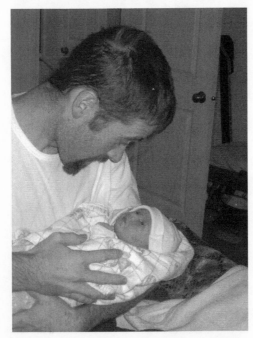

Dad and Baby Lydia (June 18, 2009)

Jacob's Grave (2010)

Caleb and Clayton in Their Baseball Gear (2010)

Glacier National Park Hike (2010)

Lacey and Lydia Dressed for Easter (2011)

Mom and Lydia (2012)

Children in San Diego (2012)

Cole Family (2012)